Mountaintop Moments

Mountaintop Moments: Meeting God in the High Places

Mountaintop Moments:
Meeting God in the High Places

978-1-5018-8401-6
978-1-5018-8402-3 eBook

Mountaintop Moments:
Meeting God in the High Places / Leader Guide

978-1-5018-8403-0
978-1-5018-8404-7 eBook

Mountaintop Moments:
Meeting God in the High Places / DVD

978-1-5018-8405-4

Also from Ed Robb:

The Wonder of Christmas: Once You Believe, Anything Is Possible (with Rob Renfroe)
Under Wraps: The Gift We Never Expected (with Jessica LaGrone, Andy Nixon, and Rob Renfroe)

MOUNTAINTOP MOMENTS

MEETING GOD IN THE HIGH PLACES

ED ROBB

Abingdon Press / Nashville

Mountaintop Moments
Meeting God in the High Places

Library of Congress Cataloging-in-Publication data has been requested.

ISBN 978-1-5018-8401-6
ISBN 978-1-5018-8402-3 ebook

19 20 21 22 23 24 25 26 27 28 — 10 9 8 7 6 5 4 3 2 1

MANUFACTURED IN THE UNITED STATES OF AMERICA

To Bev,
the love of my life.

CONTENTS

BASE CAMP

Listen, my children, and you shall hear
Of the midnight ride of Paul Revere,
On the eighteenth of April, in Seventy-Five;
Hardly a man is now alive
Who remembers that famous day and year.

He said to his friend, "If the British march
By land or sea from the town to-night,
Hang a lantern aloft in the belfry-arch
Of the North-Church-tower, as a signal-light,

One if by land, and two if by sea;
And I on the opposite shore will be,
Ready to ride and spread the alarm
Through every Middlesex village and farm,
For the country-folk to be up and to arm."[1]

These words from Henry Wadsworth Longfellow's poem "Paul Revere's Ride" intrigued me when I was a boy. Such action and suspense! The poem tells the story of an impending attack by the British Army in April of 1775. It's a creative chronicle of the events that immediately led up to the Revolutionary War. A churchman was posted in a high place—the steeple tower of the Old North Church in Boston—to alert the patriots of the enemy's approach.

A signal code using lanterns had been established—one lantern in the steeple would signal the British army's choice of the land route, while two lanterns would signal the route "by sea" across the Charles River. When the American patriot Paul Revere observed the two-lantern signal from his lookout post, he mounted his horse immediately and made a daring midnight ride through the countryside to warn his fellow patriots and call them to arms.

What about this adventure wouldn't capture the imagination of a young boy from West Texas? It was splendid. On the dusty, windswept plains where I grew up, high places were in short supply. A church steeple would surely have been the highest place around—a good place from which to signal important, life-saving messages to the people living nearby. And we did have a church in our little town. On Sunday mornings I sat and listened as my dad, a Methodist pastor, told fascinating stories about how God delivered important, lifesaving messages to his people from the high places in the Old and New Testaments. Not from church steeples but from *mountaintops*.

Some of my happiest childhood memories come from time spent in the mountains on family vacations. Our family didn't live near any mountains; not even close. The nearest mountain range was the Rocky Mountains, and getting there wasn't easy. It required a long, hot two days of traveling. And there were *seven* of us crammed into the car—my parents and five children. As you can imagine, that made for a very long trip! But we made the effort. We knew the experience would be worth it.

Something within us calls us to the mountains, doesn't it? Maybe it's the fresh air that fills our lungs and helps to clear our minds. Perhaps the higher elevations help us gain perspective in our lives. Certainly our view changes—we are treated to a panoramic revelation of what cannot be seen from the ground. And sometimes that revelation can speak to us in a deeper sense. Whatever calls us, there seems to be an innate sense of God's presence when we climb to a high place—as if somehow we draw closer to the Almighty because we are nearer the heavens. The psalmist tells us:

> *From heaven the Lᴏʀᴅ looks down*
> *and sees all mankind;*
> *from his dwelling place he watches*
> *all who live on earth—*
> *he who forms the hearts of all,*
> *who considers everything they do.*
>
> *(Psalm 33:13-15)*

Since the beginning of biblical history, mountains have played a great role in the story of our faith. God always knew where the enemy was encamped. As he watched over the journeys of his beloved chosen people, he knew when their paths were straight and faithful and knew when they were being led astray. And when God needed to offer correction, strategy, encouragement, or life-saving warnings, he often signaled his children from a mountaintop.

> *Now Moses was keeping the flock of his father-in-law, Jethro, the priest of Midian, and he led his flock to the west side of the wilderness and came to Horeb, the mountain of God. And the angel of the Lᴏʀᴅ appeared to him in a flame of fire out of the midst of a bush. He looked, and behold, the bush was burning, yet it was not consumed. And Moses said, "I will turn aside to see this great sight, why the bush is not burned."*
>
> *(Exodus 3:1-3 ESV)*

I will turn aside. Just as God did with Moses, whenever he desired an encounter with his people, he sent a signal to turn them aside—to *look up* and *come up* into his presence to receive his message. Throughout the Old and New Testaments, Scripture tells us God has signaled his people from the mountaintops with his voice, fire, thunder, clouds, and in person—in the life and ministry of Jesus Christ.

In this book we will turn aside to encounter our God on several important mountaintops. Our journey will take us through two Middle Eastern countries and through both the Old and New Testaments of the Bible—from the days of Abraham to the time of Jesus—more than two millennia. Some of these summits might be quite steep, but together we will make the effort. The experience will be worth it.

To encourage each of you as we set out together, I offer this prayer as written in Scripture:

> *I lift up my eyes to the mountains—*
> *where does my help come from?*
> *My help comes from the LORD,*
> *the Maker of heaven and earth.*
>
> *He will not let your foot slip—*
> *he who watches over you will not slumber;*
> *indeed, he who watches over Israel*
> *will neither slumber nor sleep.*
>
> *The LORD watches over you—*
> *the LORD is your shade at your right hand;*
> *the sun will not harm you by day,*
> *nor the moon by night.*
>
> *The LORD will keep you from all harm—*
> *he will watch over your life;*
> *the LORD will watch over your coming and going*
> *both now and forevermore.*
>
> *(Psalm 121)*

Ready to leave Base Camp? Let's begin our ascent.

1

MORIAH: MOUNT OF PROVISION

Delight yourself in the Lord,
and he will give you the desires of your heart.

Commit your way to the Lord;
trust in him, and he will act.

(Psalm 37:4-5 ESV)

As we begin our journey, I'd first like to make a stop to visit an iconic symbol of our nation. Our trip takes us deep into the Black Hills of South Dakota, where we enter the Mount Rushmore National Memorial. Four sixty-foot-tall faces set into the mountain's granite peak create quite the breathtaking display. A quick test before you read on—do you know the identity of these four figures?

If you answered that the faces are those of four presidents—George Washington, Thomas Jefferson, Theodore Roosevelt, and Abraham Lincoln—you'd be correct. This awe-inspiring memorial features the visage of leaders who are believed to represent the birth, growth, development, and preservation of our country.

With this in mind, what if we had a scriptural Mount Rushmore? Which great leaders represent the birth, growth, development, and

13

preservation of our faith; and whose faces might be carved into this mountain?

Setting Jesus aside for a moment, let's start with the New Testament. Who would *you* put on a scriptural Mount Rushmore?

Two of the apostles come to my mind immediately—Peter and Paul. Not only did Peter walk on water literally, but Jesus also proclaimed that Peter was the rock upon which he would build his church (Matthew 16:18). Paul wrote the letters that comprise half of the New Testament and are primarily responsible for bringing the good news of the gospel of Jesus Christ to both Jew and Gentile.

Who would represent the Old Testament on our scriptural Mount Rushmore? This may be more difficult to narrow, since the Old Testament is home to so many giants of our faith. Moses? Elijah? David? Or maybe Isaiah?

We certainly can't leave out Abraham—the one whom God chose to begin the restoration of an intimate relationship with humankind. God even refers to Abraham as his *friend* in Isaiah 41:8. Following Yahweh's personal, divine calling, Abraham began to practice monotheism, the belief and worship of one God, and rejected the pagan, polytheistic culture that surrounded him. He is uniquely claimed as the father of three faiths—Judaism, Christianity, and Islam.

Yes, Abraham deserves a place on our scriptural Mount Rushmore. The story of his fascinating life and relationship with the Almighty is found in the Book of Genesis and is set in the mountainous region of Moriah, in ancient Israel.

Have you ever investigated your genealogy? Maybe you have tried one of those DNA tests from ancestry websites. Maybe you discovered something surprising about where your ancestors came from or even to whom you are distantly related; for instance, a former US president, famous actor, or even royalty.

Abraham's interesting genealogy is laid out carefully in

Genesis chapters 5, 10, and 11. He was a direct descendant of another pivotal figure in biblical history: a man who was obedient to God—a man who built an ark—a man named Noah. Noah had three sons: Shem, Ham, and Japheth. Abraham, first known as Abram, was born through the generations of Shem.

As we read through the stories in Genesis about the lives of Noah and Abraham, we discover several striking similarities in the character of these two men. Both were obedient to God. Both trusted God. Both answered God's call, even when the call seemed impossible. And these stories also reveal a pattern that points to the very character of God himself.

We learn that it is God who takes the initiative; God who pursues us; God who is working for our salvation; God who is giving us his promise; and God who is making plans for our provision. As New Testament people, we already know the end of this story. Right? The salvation story: God's mighty plan for redemption, which culminates in the life, death, and resurrection of Jesus Christ.

But God began the salvation story thousands of years earlier, when he called Abraham. Genesis chapters 11–21 teach us that Abraham was a man who was called to follow God. A man with whom God made a covenant. A man whose offspring was promised to be too numerous to count. A man who would live a life of obedience.

Now, in chapter 22, we find Abraham in the land of Moriah. Abraham had been faithfully following God. He had heard God speak to him, promising he would have an heir and that his offspring would be more numerous than the grains of sand on the earth or the stars in the sky. But a lot of time had passed since Abraham first heard that promise, and he began to doubt and question God. I can just imagine his prayerful conversations with the Almighty: "God, I have no son to call my own, to bear my name, no son with my wife Sarah. You said you had a plan. You said my descendants would be as numerous as the stars, and I thought it was a good plan. I was all in. But now I'm one hundred years old."

Abraham doubted, yet Isaac was born.

God also spoke to Abraham's wife, Sarah. I imagine their conversation went a similar way. God promised Sarah, "I will give you a son." Sarah replied, "Let's get real, God. I'm ninety years old, way past the childbearing years—it's not going to happen."

Sarah doubted, yet Isaac was born.

Our doubts, however justified, do not block God's provision, and his provision often comes suddenly. In a miraculous moment, everything changes.

Do you know anyone who has had a surprise baby? I'm referring to the couple whose children are teenagers, or off to college, and then suddenly, out of the blue, a baby is on the way! There's a spontaneous cry of "How did this happen?" They never imagined! They find themselves in shock. Maybe they even sink into a bit of a depression and worry, *People will think we are the child's grandparents!* Maybe you know a couple in a similar situation; and yet, after their child is born, their feelings take a wonderful and remarkable turn. The shock and fear turn into the greatest blessing of their lives that brings with it a love that is simply indescribable. That's what happened to Abraham and Sarah.

When the situation seemed humanly impossible, that's when God acted. He had a divine plan, and he made divine provision. At long last, Abraham and Sarah had a son, whom they named Isaac. Even the meaning of his name, "He laughs," points to the incredulity of his parents when told they would have a son at their advanced ages . . . they laughed! And now, instead of laughing with incredulity, they laughed with joy.

As time passed, and Isaac grew, don't you know Abraham and Sarah were devoted parents! They made sure Isaac had all the advantages. They dressed him in the latest Gap for Desert Kids clothing. They put him in the local Music for Little Methuselahs program. They led the cheering section at every one of his sheepshearing or camel-racing contests. They undoubtedly taught him about the God of Abraham, who had miraculously brought Isaac into their lives. Without question, Sarah and Abraham loved this boy deeply.

Then, suddenly, in the middle of this wonderful love story, God spoke to Abraham again. Genesis 22:1-2 tells us,

> *Some time later God tested Abraham. He said to him, "Abraham!"*
>
> *"Here I am," he replied.*
>
> *Then God said, "Take your son, your only son, whom you love—Isaac—and go to the region of Moriah. Sacrifice him there as a burnt offering on a mountain I will show you."*

Just when everything was going along great, God *tested* Abraham. God tested his obedience; God tested his heart; and God tested his priorities. That's a sobering thought, isn't it? God actually *tests* us? I thought I was out of school—finished with testing. Are you telling me that there are tests in life? *Divine* tests? I'm not sure I like that idea.

Abraham was indeed tested, and Scripture tells us he has not been the only one. Consider for a moment the Israelites. When we read the story of the Exodus, we see they also were tested. God called Moses and sent him back to Egypt with a message: *Tell the pharaoh to let my people go.*

You know the story. God dramatically rescued his Hebrew children from slavery under the pharaoh. But achieving that freedom wasn't so easy. Leaving prosperous Egypt to wander out into the unknown wilderness—*that* was scary! Following the God of

Abraham meant they had to leave all that they knew—the guarantee of food and housing—and lean on God's provision. The Israelites had to learn to trust God, to walk by faith. In truth, they were God's chosen people, but they didn't always trust him. They were saved by God's mighty acts, but they didn't always remember. God promised the Israelites a land of their own, one flowing with milk and honey, but they didn't always believe this promise. In this time of testing, the Israelites reacted in typical human fashion—with doubt, unbelief, and fear.

> *All the Israelites grumbled against Moses and Aaron, and the whole assembly said to them, "If only we had died in Egypt! Or in this wilderness! Why is the LORD bringing us to this land only to let us fall by the sword? Our wives and children will be taken as plunder. Wouldn't it be better for us to go back to Egypt?"*
>
> *(Numbers 14:2-3)*

These stories in Scripture teach us that one thing is certain—tests in life will come. Circumstances, troubles, relationships, and even our own children will test us. And, like the Hebrews of old, we don't always pass these tests. We don't always trust. We don't always believe. Our courage fails. Our faith grows timid.

The reality is, in the school of life we will all be tested. Even Jesus was tested. At the beginning of his ministry, he was led by the Spirit into the wilderness to be tempted by the devil for forty days. But Jesus remained faithful to the word and will of his Father throughout his temptation and triumphed over Satan's efforts (Matthew 4:1-11). Then there was that heartbreaking night in the garden of Gethsemane. Jesus knew the Jewish authorities were after him. He knew the Romans would arrest him. He knew the crowds would turn on him. He knew his own disciples would desert him. *He knew the cross lay ahead of him.*

That night the garden of Gethsemane became a battleground for Jesus' soul. Matthew tells us of his mighty struggle to stay true and his pleas for strength: "Going a little farther, he fell with his face to the ground and prayed, 'My Father, if it is possible, may this cup be taken from me. Yet not as I will, but as you will'" (26:39).

If anyone can understand how difficult these times of testing in life are, Jesus can. His struggles were real, just like ours, and how he dealt with them gives us a basis for courage. Life will test us over and over again. With each test, we arrive at a crossroads—either we trust God's provision and trust God's word, increasing our faith, or we remain enslaved by fear and doubt. Life would be so much easier if we didn't have to go through trying times at all. Being tested is uncomfortable, but this is how character is formed and how faith is developed.

I wish I could say that I have always passed the tests that come my way, but I haven't. And I suspect you haven't either. There have been times in my life when I haven't trusted. There have been times when my prayers have been weak; times when fears and anxieties got the best of me. At times I didn't resist temptation; I didn't say no to sin's lure. There have been times when I wasn't able to believe in God's provision and times when I didn't put his calling first. I could very well place myself in that crowd of doubting, complaining Israelites wandering in the desert after the Exodus.

We find hope in knowing that the great men and women of Scripture (the ones we would put on the scriptural Mount Rushmore) didn't always pass the test either. But God never gave up on them. And God won't give up on you. He tests us, not to fail us, but to teach us to depend on him—to trust *him* more than we trust ourselves—to know we can rely on his word, his promises, and his provision.

Let's return to Abraham's story. When God told Abraham that he and Sarah would have a son, did Abraham trust and believe? No, he laughed; but Isaac was born. Then it became a little easier to trust and believe. Abraham's faith must have grown through that experience, don't you think? For Abraham's next big test, God asked him to do the unthinkable. And Abraham passed with flying colors.

> *Then God said, "Take your son, your only son, whom you love—Isaac—and go to the region of Moriah. Sacrifice him there as a burnt offering on a mountain I will show you."*
>
> *(Genesis 22:2)*

Sacrifice him there. I can hardly imagine what went through Abraham's mind. *No! Not Isaac. Surely you won't ask me to sacrifice our son. You didn't give us this boy, in our old age, only to take him from us! This precious child who carries your promise of descendants more numerous than stars and sands. Not Isaac!*

We will never know all the thoughts that raced through Abraham's mind that day. But what we do know is this: *Abraham obeyed.* And his response was immediate. Genesis 22 tells us further:

> *Early the next morning Abraham got up and loaded his donkey. He took with him two of his servants and his son Isaac. When he had cut enough wood for the burnt offering, he set out for the place God had told him about. On the third day Abraham looked up and saw the place in the distance. He said to his servants, "Stay here with the donkey while I and the boy go over there. We will worship and then we will come back to you."*
>
> *(Genesis 22:3-5)*

Where is the dialogue between God and Abraham? Where was the questioning? The arguing? *There wasn't any.* Abraham simply got up and obeyed.

Abraham's pure obedience is hard for us to fathom. But then we remember that by this time, Abraham had walked with God a long time, and he knew God could be trusted. If Abraham had had the opportunity to write a psalm of the heart during this difficult journey to Moriah, I imagine it may have looked like this:

I don't understand what's going on here, LORD.
I can't make sense of your direction.
I thought the whole purpose of sending this miracle
child was to bring forth spiritual descendants.
To begin a great nation of your people.

People called by your Name. And through them,
all people on earth will be blessed.
No, LORD. I don't understand your ways.
Still, I will follow.
Still, I will trust.
Still, I will obey.

And that's exactly what Abraham did. He followed God. He trusted God. He obeyed God, and he *worshiped* God.

Abraham had a remarkable faith, forged in the successes—and failures—of the many previous life tests he had endured.

Worshiping God had become a lifelong pattern for Abraham, and he marked each spiritual milestone of his walk with the Almighty by building an altar. When God called Abraham, when God gave him land, and when God promised him descendants, Abraham built an altar. Upon these altars, Abraham sacrificed his own will to the will of God; and, by doing so, he experienced God's provision—a friendship with God, a new land that would become the nation of Israel, and a true son by his beloved Sarah.

Over and over, Abraham had experienced this divine provision, and his natural response was to worship—to give thanks to his God. So it's not surprising to hear Abraham tell his servants that he and his son, Isaac, were going to continue up Mount Moriah to worship God and build an altar.

Now, building an altar to worship God—that's one thing. But sacrificing your beloved son on that same altar—that's quite another. It's a horrifying thought. You and I cry out and ask, *How could Abraham do this? How could he sacrifice his own son?* Our minds can't make sense of it. What kind of vengeful, wrathful, wretched God *is* this God of the Old Testament?

But the truth *is* horrifying—child sacrifice was common in many of the pagan cultures of Abraham's day. Abraham lived more than four thousand years ago—two thousand years before Christ. For some of the cultures at that time, life was cheap. It would not have been shocking for Abraham, or any of his peers, to think that their god would require human sacrifice. That was normal. That was the kind of world in which Abraham lived.

Thankfully, a marvelous truth begins to reveal itself in Abraham's story. Abraham was God's called-out one. In essence God was saying, "Abraham, you and your descendants are not going to live like all those other people—those tribes that surround you. You're not going to bow down before their gods and worship the way they worship." So God called Abraham to the mountaintop at Moriah, not for him to practice human sacrifice, but to teach him that his God was different; God alone provides the sacrifice. And there's more to the great truth taught at Mount Moriah. God didn't want Abraham to give his son as an offering. God wanted Abraham to offer his own life at the altar.

What does that mean? It means not holding anything back. Giving God every part of our life—even the part that is most precious to us. It means giving God our future and trusting in his provision.

Put on Abraham's sandals, and imagine hiking up that mountain with your son—the child who is so precious to you. As you climb, the little boy carries the wood obediently. He loves you. He trusts you. He likes being with you. You walk along together, mostly in silence. And then your son innocently asks: "Father? . . . The fire and wood are here, . . . but where is the lamb for the burnt offering?" (Genesis 22:7).

The struggle and sorrow that Abraham experienced that night and on the journey to the mountain those next three days must have been intense. Moriah had truly become a battleground for his soul. How difficult it must have been to keep his voice round and full when his little boy asked, "Dad, where is the sacrifice?" In a powerful profession of faith, Abraham simply answered, "God himself will provide the lamb for the burnt offering, my son" (verse 8). And the two of them went on together to the place where God had sent them.

When they reached their destination, Abraham built an altar, laid the wood and coals for the fire, and then bound his precious son and placed him on the altar. Imagine the fear and shock when the boy realized *he* was to be the sacrifice! God commanded Abraham to sacrifice his son to teach Abraham the lessons of obedience and trust. In doing so, Abraham was teaching his son the greatest lesson you can ever teach a child—to obey God. Period. No matter the cost.

How conflicting it must have seemed. First, it took every bit of faith Abraham could muster in his heart to believe God's promise of Abraham's future descendants who would possess and bless the land. And now that faith is nearly shattered by God's apparent attempt to destroy his promise. If he were to obey God in this terrible moment, what would become of the promise? The hope?

But Abraham's faith withstood the test. He trusted and obeyed, even when God's ways seemed impossibly contradictory.

Let's continue in the story. Slowly, Abraham piled wood onto the altar. There was no sign of a miracle from God. Slowly, he bound his boy, Isaac, and laid him upon it. Slowly, he unsheathed the knife and still no sign. Abraham lifted his hand to sacrifice his son. Then suddenly, God made an appearance.

*But the angel of the L*ORD *called out to him from heaven, "Abraham! Abraham!"*

"Here I am," he replied.

"Do not lay a hand on the boy," he said. "Do not do anything to him. Now I know that you fear God, because you have not withheld from me your son, your only son."

Abraham looked up and there in a thicket he saw a ram caught by its horns.

(Genesis 22:11-13)

In a miraculous moment, everything changed. Isaac was released. The ram was substituted. The burnt offering was made. And when the sacrifice was finished, Abraham named this place *Jehovah Jireh,* "The LORD Will Provide." This was not a name that reminded him of his trial but a name that proclaimed God's deliverance. Abraham wanted this altar on Mount Moriah to be remembered not for his sufferings but for God's faithfulness.

What about the mountaintop altars we have built in our own lives? I'm certain that you have experienced many impossible challenges and struggles in your life journey, just as I have, and have names for them. Are they names that recall our suffering, or do they shine a light on God's blessings?

I'm reminded of when Queen Elizabeth II announced to the world that she was naming 1992 an *annus horribilis*—a horrible year. Her daughter, Princess Anne, divorced. The queen's sons, Prince Andrew and Prince Charles, the heir to the throne, announced separations from their spouses that year. Charles's wife, Diana, secretly cooperated for a tell-all book about her unhappy marriage. And one of the queen's primary residences suffered a terrible fire. Yes, it was a bad year, and she gave it a name: *Annus Horribilis.*

I wonder, if we were to examine the most difficult times in our own lives, would we view them purely as miserable experiences? Or might our perspective from the top of the mountain shift our perception to see God's faithfulness in the midst of our trials?

Abraham chose to name God's faithfulness and said, "The Lord will provide."

We can learn an important lesson from Abraham's story—to speak boldly what we believe God has promised to do in our lives, just as Abraham did. It is a powerful expression of faith, bringing us into agreement with the One who provides. Many of you already know firsthand the truth dramatically taught at Mount Moriah. God listens to our prayers. And God provides. In his time. In his way.

I was reminded of this truth on a recent trip to India. I was in Dehradun, in the foothills of the Himalayas. My wife, Beverley, and I traveled to that remote location with our church's missions pastor. Our purpose for the long journey was to participate in the dedication of the new library at Luther New Theological College, the building for which our church had provided the primary funds.

At dinner that first evening, while visiting around the table, the conversation turned to the interesting story of one new student, a seventeen-year-old girl named Poonam. The school's founder, Dr. George Chavanikamannil, told us that Poonam had applied to enroll in the school of music as a piano major. Her exams and credentials were both exceptional. But competition for these programs is fierce, and the music program was completely full. With regret, the academic dean sent Poonam a rejection letter, explaining there were no more openings and warmly invited her to reapply for admission the next year.

Poonam appealed in a letter back to the dean, saying she had won a full scholarship for one year but if not accepted she would lose the scholarship to another student. Again, the dean responded with the sad news that it was simply not possible and instructed her not to come.

Two days before the fall semester began, the young woman showed up on campus. Her parents drove her the long distance from their village and dropped her off, with her meager belongings, completely unannounced. Then her parents left without speaking to anyone. They literally abandoned her at the school.

Once young people become Christians, their Hindu families reject them. Such was the case with several students at the school, including Poonam. The school was heartbroken but had no options. They had no room for her. Poonam continued to pray, pleading for the Lord to make a way—to open a door for her—any door.

The school administrators agreed to house and feed her for a couple of weeks until somehow they could return her back to her home in the hopes her parents' hearts might soften. Poonam wept and prayed continuously. She believed in a God who provides.

Then a miracle happened. Dr. Chavanikamannil received an email from a young woman in Indiana, a gifted musician and educator. This Christian professor had shown interest in joining the faculty the previous year and was a perfect fit for their needs. However, the bureaucratic slowness of the Indian government and their strong prejudice against granting visas had been so discouraging that the music professor finally gave up. But in the email to Dr. Chavanikamannil, the professor said that over the last few days she had strongly felt God's prompting, and she now was determined to persevere and come to India. She could arrive by spring semester if the position was still open and if she was still needed.

Upon learning this news, several already exhausted and overloaded music professors agreed to work yet longer, so Poonam could receive private piano instruction until her new professor arrived in the spring.

Thanks be to God! The power of persistent prayers. God opened a door for his beloved daughter. *Jehovah Jireh.* God provides.

While Abraham's powerful story speaks to his unwavering faithfulness and God's abhorrence of child sacrifice, above all it teaches us about God's great love for humankind. Abraham and Isaac's experience on Mount Moriah provides us with an early, divine insight into the restorative workings of God throughout human history—throughout both biblical testaments. The Old Testament land of Moriah—Abraham's mount of provision—is known in the New Testament and in present day as Jerusalem.

Abraham's beloved son, Isaac, foreshadows the coming of Christ. Isaac—the long-promised, miraculously born son—was an unwilling participant in the events on Mount Moriah. Jesus Christ—the long-promised, miraculously born Son—was a willing participant in the events on Mount Calvary. Isaac carried wood to Mount Moriah. Jesus carried his wooden cross to Mount Calvary. Isaac's hands and feet were bound on the altar. Jesus' hands and feet were nailed to the cross. But one glaring difference stands between these two. Isaac was delivered. Christ was crucified.

What God would not allow Abraham to do, he did himself. The God of provision provided a ram for the sacrifice so that Isaac could be saved. What we, as beloved children, are unable to do for ourselves, God did for us. The God of provision sacrificed his own son, Jesus Christ, so that we might be forgiven and saved.

> *For God so loved the world that he gave his one and only Son, that whoever believes in him shall not perish but have eternal life.*
> *(John 3:16)*

Thanks be to God!

PEAK PERSPECTIVES: ARARAT

One thousand miles northeast of Mount Moriah in modern-day Turkey sits a formidable mountain named Ararat. Volcanic in origin, Ararat rises steeply out of the plains to a towering 16,000 feet. In size, these two mountains are quite different; but biblically, they are strikingly similar. Upon these mountains, two ancient ancestors learned that obedience to the Creator God brings life-giving blessing.

Noah, a righteous man in a horribly sinful and corrupt world, was favored by God and selected to carry the human race through a devastating purge. When Noah was five hundred years old, he was instructed to build an ark . . . in the middle of the desert . . . where it never rains. We can only imagine the confusion, incredulity, and doubt that must have run through Noah's mind as God gave him detailed instructions. But Noah loved God and trusted him. And so he obeyed. Scripture tells us it took nearly one hundred years to build the monstrous ark, and certainly Noah had moments of weakness—he surely was ridiculed for this strange undertaking. Yet with steadfast faith and resolve, Noah, with the help of his three sons—Shem, Ham, and Japheth—built the ark, down to the last detail. It was ready.

> *When everything was ready, the LORD said to Noah, "Go into the boat with all your family, for among all the people of the earth, I can see that you alone are righteous. Take with you seven pairs—male and female—of each animal I have approved for eating and for sacrifice, and take one pair of each of the others. Also take seven pairs of every kind of bird. There must be a male and a female in each pair to ensure that all life will survive on the earth after the flood. Seven days from now I will make the rains pour down on the earth. And it will rain for forty days and forty nights, until I have wiped from the earth all the living things I have created."*
>
> *So Noah did everything as the LORD commanded him.*
>
> (Genesis 7:1-5 NLT)

Can you imagine how Noah felt when the first raindrop fell in the desert? The fear. The knowledge that God was really going to do just what he said he was going to do. The thankfulness he had remained steadfast and faithful . . . against all odds.

The rains fell for forty days and forty nights and wiped out all life on the earth. For one hundred fifty days Noah's ark floated on the floodwaters and finally ran aground on the mountain named Ararat. As the waters receded, God blessed Noah and his family, saying, "Be fruitful and increase in number and fill the earth" (Genesis 9:1). Noah's obedience brought the blessing of life to him, his family, and the multitude of generations to follow him.

Four hundred years later, Noah's descendant, Abraham, climbed Mount Moriah in an act of obedience that defied all odds. God had asked Abraham—his friend—to sacrifice his beloved son,

Isaac. We can only imagine the confusion, incredulity, and doubt that must have run through Abraham's mind as God gave this command. But Abraham loved and trusted God, and in an act of remarkable faith, he obeyed.

Up on that mountain, at the very last instant, God stayed Abraham's hand.

> *"Do not lay a hand on the boy," he said. "Do not do anything to him. Now I know that you fear God, because you have not withheld from me your son, your only son."*
>
> *Abraham looked up and there in a thicket he saw a ram caught by its horns. He went over and took the ram and sacrificed it as a burnt offering instead of his son. So Abraham called that place The LORD Will Provide. And to this day it is said, "On the mountain of the LORD it will be provided."*
> *(Genesis 22:12-14)*

Abraham's obedience resulted in life-giving blessings. His beloved son, Isaac, was spared. God blessed Abraham for his obedience and promised his offspring would be more numerous than the stars. We—you and I—are counted among those stars. And we are the beneficiaries of the miraculous provision of the sacrifice on Mount Moriah. The ram sacrificed for Abraham's beloved son, Isaac, was a picture of the sacrifice that was to come for all humankind—the sacrifice of God's beloved son, Jesus the Christ.

The ancient winds carried from Ararat and Moriah call us to obedience. When we answer in faith, our reward is the blessing of life—everlasting life.

2

SINAI: MOUNT
OF GOD'S LAW

"Listen to me, my people.
Hear me, Israel,
for my law will be proclaimed,
and my justice will become a light to the nations.
My mercy and justice are coming soon.
My salvation is on the way."
(Isaiah 51:4-5 NLT)

Several years ago my wife and I traveled with a group to Israel and Mount Sinai. We crossed the Israeli border into Egypt at Eilat, on the Red Sea. From there it was a long journey across the wilderness through some of the most barren, desolate landscape I've ever seen. And mind you, I grew up in West Texas.

For me, it was an emotional moment as I saw the mountain called Sinai rising from the desert floor. Mount Sinai isn't all that tall, as mountains go—just 7,500 feet. Yet it towers above all the other mountains of the Old Testament because it is the place where Moses went to meet God.

Upon our arrival we spent the night in simple quarters near the base of this famous mountain. We were all exhausted from the long trip, which began in Jerusalem. Retiring to bed, as rudimentary as our accommodations were, never seemed so inviting. By midnight, however, we were already out of our tents and mounting the backs of camels. Our goal? To ascend the mountain and arrive at the summit before dawn in order to watch the sun rise from the desert floor. This same desert, which had been so inhospitably hot by day, was now surprisingly cold.

Once we reached Sinai's summit, we waited. It was so quiet. I marveled that we were standing in the place where God spoke to Moses and the Israelites amid thunder and clouds and fire. As I shivered from the cold, I was struck by the realization we were engulfed in absolute darkness. There was no ambient light in this desolate wilderness. In our modern day, we have forgotten what complete darkness is like. And, quite possibly, part of the reason for my shivers could be attributed to the knowledge that we were truly standing on holy ground.

Finally the sun began to rise. It started as just a glow on the horizon. Then a golden-red sliver appeared; and soon the sky was filled with the piercing brilliance of a full morning sun. In those glorious moments, light poured out into the wilderness. The darkness was gone.

Three thousand years ago, Moses descended from Mount Sinai after his meeting with God. His face shone so brightly with the reflected light of God's presence that the people were afraid to come near him (Exodus 34:29-30). Moses carried in his arms the two tablets of testimony—the Law—that would pour the light of God's grace into the world. Commandments sent from heaven, not to restrict us, but to free us—from the absolute darkness called sin.

Isn't it interesting how we call spiritually high experiences in our lives "mountaintop moments"? Maybe it's because we equate being on the mountaintop with being close to God—like Moses—as though we are nearer to heaven. And we want that, don't we—to be connected to our Creator? It's the way we're wired. We want to be close to God and feel that God has a part in our lives. We want to hear from God; but the irony is, we only want to hear the good stuff. We want to hear God tell us, "I accept you. I love you. You're forgiven. I'll comfort you. I'm here to help you. I'll provide for all your needs." We don't reach out hoping to hear God say, "Don't do that. Don't go there. Don't succumb to that temptation. Don't hang out with that crowd." We want our mountaintop moments to be all about freedom and feeling good. But as we look at the story of Mount Sinai in Scripture, we discover that sometimes those critical mountaintop moments in our lives need to be about boundaries.

I imagine many of you, like me, can recall scenes from the classic movie *The Ten Commandments*.[1] Moses, portrayed by actor Charlton Heston, stands atop a boulder at the Red Sea, with his hair blowing in the wind, and stretches his staff over the waters that are about to part. Later, Moses stands on Mount Sinai, holding two stone tablets while he overlooks the rebellious Israelites, his hair now snow-white from his encounter with God. Hollywood's drama and special effects are impressive; yet they pale in comparison to the Israelites' real-life encounter with God at Sinai as described in the Book of Exodus.

Being obedient to God's call, Moses led the Hebrew people out of the bondage of slavery under the Egyptian pharaoh. God guided and protected them as they fled through the wilderness of Egypt and gave them miraculous, safe passage through the waters of the Red Sea. Three months after their escape from the pharaoh, they arrived at Mount Sinai.

Great is the significance of the wandering route the Israel-ites took that landed them in the remote, desolate Sinai wilder-ness. Instead of traveling due east, the shortest route to the

Promised Land, they traveled southeast to the Red Sea and then further south to Sinai. Why the long, arduous route through the inhospitable desert? Because their Creator wanted to meet with them privately about things that were crucial to their survival. The Israelites were God's chosen people—a people he had set apart to be a holy nation.

However, these people did not know how to be a holy nation. They had been enslaved four hundred years to a pharaoh in an alien land that served alien gods, far from the Promised Land that God had given to them. Life had been exceedingly harsh—the pharaoh was a cruel taskmaster. And the Israelites were a discouraged people. They had all but forgotten God. To them, the God of Abraham, Isaac, Jacob, and Joseph was more a distant memory than a present reality. His power was forgotten. His purpose was forgotten. Even after fleeing to freedom in the desert, the Israelites were more afraid of the future than they were of the past. They had no idea how to govern, protect, or provide for themselves. They wanted to go back to Egypt. Life had broken their spirit to the point they had forgotten who they were—the beloved children of God. So they were drawn aside for a divinely arranged appointment on the mountain with their Creator.

Have you ever felt the way these discouraged, confused Israelites did? Maybe life has been hard on you. Maybe you're trapped in the bondage of sin, and there seems to be no hope for escape. Maybe all of life's experiences shout to you that you're not important—that your value is measured only by your labor—that your destiny is already settled and you're a "loser." Maybe you believe you're not worthy of being loved. Maybe you think God has given up on you or has forgotten you altogether.

Don't believe it! Remember, you are a child of God, and you are infinitely precious to him. You may be faithless, but God is faithful.

And he hears the cry of your heart, just as he heard the cries of his children hiding in the Egyptian desert.

Let's reenter the story by joining Moses and the Israelites in the Sinai wilderness. As God's children camped at the base of the mountain, he decided to speak to them, and he summoned Moses up the mountain to meet him. I can only imagine what thoughts were going through the minds of the Israelites as they watched their leader walk slowly up the steep mountain and become enveloped by a formidable cloud. Would they ever see him again? Would they be left alone in this grueling wilderness to fend for themselves?

When Moses had climbed the mountain, God spoke to him and reminded him of the grace that had brought the Hebrews to this place and of their restoration that was to come:

> "'You yourselves have seen what I did to Egypt, and how I carried you on eagles' wings and brought you to myself. Now if you obey me fully and keep my covenant, then out of all nations you will be my treasured possession. Although the whole earth is mine, you will be for me a kingdom of priests and a holy nation.'"
>
> (Exodus 19:4-6)

Then he told Moses to go back down and tell the people to consecrate and cleanse themselves—to prepare to meet their holy God. The Israelites were about to experience a much-needed mountaintop moment.

> On the morning of the third day there was thunder and lightning, with a thick cloud over the mountain, and a very loud trumpet blast. Everyone in the camp trembled. Then Moses led the people out of the camp to meet with God, and they stood at the foot of the mountain. Mount Sinai was covered with smoke, because the LORD descended on it

in fire. The smoke billowed up from it like smoke from a furnace, and the whole mountain trembled violently.

(Exodus 19:16-18)

God spoke in the thunder, warning the people to not come up the mountain, for it was a holy place. Anyone who disobeyed would perish (Exodus 19:19-22). In that moment God reaffirmed who he is to this wayward group of former Hebrew slaves. He is the one and only true God—the God of Abraham, Isaac, Jacob, and Joseph—the great I AM. He was also setting boundaries. He was holy, and they were not.

Have you ever heard the expression "the fear of God"? Perhaps as a child you were doing something forbidden, and your mother or grandmother shook her finger at you and said, "If you don't stop right now, I'll put the fear of God in you!" Most likely, hearing the words *fear* and *God* used together in the same sentence was enough to make you comply immediately with her demand. Scripture tells us that everyone who was at Sinai in the presence of God that day trembled. The fire, clouds, trumpet blasts, and thunderous voice of God restored the *fear of God*—the reverential respect and desire to comply in order to avoid the judgment of the holy and mighty Creator—within the Israelites.

As Israel held its collective breath at the base of the mountain, God spoke again and gave Moses his Law—the Ten Commandments:

*"I am the L*ORD *your God, who brought you out of Egypt, out of the land of slavery.*

"You shall have no other gods before me.

"You shall not make for yourself an image in the form of anything in heaven above or on the earth beneath or in the waters below. . . .

> *"You shall not misuse the name of the L*ORD
> *your God. . . .*
>
> *"Remember the Sabbath day by keeping it holy."*
> *(Exodus 20:2-4, 7-8)*

These first four commandments contain the vertical part of this new covenant, the laws that shaped the children of Israel's relationship *with God*. God is One, and God is supreme. God cannot be expressed in material form. God's name is holy. The Sabbath—the day of rest and worship— must be safeguarded.

The next six commandments change direction and provide the horizontal part of the covenant:

> *"Honor your father and your mother. . . .*
>
> *"You shall not murder.*
>
> *"You shall not commit adultery.*
>
> *"You shall not steal.*
>
> *"You shall not give false testimony against*
> *your neighbor.*
>
> *"You shall not covet . . . anything that belongs*
> *to your neighbor."*
> *(Exodus 20:12-17)*

These six are God's laws that define our relationship *with each other*, how we are to treat one another and how we are to behave. Parents are to be honored. Human life is sacred. The right of property is conserved. Sexual purity and fidelity are demanded. False and slanderous speaking about others is condemned. Coveting is wrong.

God gave Moses the Ten Commandments to set boundaries for the children of Israel and give them a way to enter into relationship with a holy God.

I can just hear the groans of the Israelites as they huddled at the base of the mountain. *More rules and regulations? We just escaped the rule of slavery. We want to be free! There might be only ten rules, but they are difficult. Nobody is perfect—we'll never measure up.*

Aren't we a bit like those Israelites, tired and discouraged by being controlled by rules? No shoes, no shirt, no service; and speed limits—especially speed limits. Long security lines and Transportation Safety Administration regulations that govern to the ounce what we are permitted to carry aboard an airplane. We live surrounded by regulations that are controlled by lawmakers and faceless bureaucrats. It seems that the government wants to control every aspect of our lives. Each year, thousands of pages of new rules, regulations, and notices are added to the Federal Register. As tiresome as this may seem, we are fortunate to have the opportunity to live freely under the law of our land, for we do not live under the rule of oppression. And although not without consequence, we still have the choice to follow the laws or not to follow them.

Admittedly, we all know how important rules and regulations are in our daily lives. They keep us safe. When our grandchildren are with us, we have rules at our house. "You cannot go in the swimming pool without me." Why? Because they might drown. "You cannot run out into the street without holding my hand." Why? Because they might get hit by a car. Just as God loves us, we love our children and grandchildren, so we set limits on what they can do—we create boundaries for their lives.

God's intention was never to oppress humanity with his Law but to provide a perfectly balanced way to relate to both heaven and our fellow human beings. Beginning with "I am the Lord your God" and ending with how we are to treat our neighbors, these ten basic commandments to live by are still very much in effect. God has never repealed them. These straightforward laws were given to the Israelites, and to us, because we are loved. They are meant to guide our steps along a straight and narrow path of righteous living.

Have you ever driven up some of those steep mountain roads in the Rocky Mountains—those impossibly narrow roads with hairpin turns? They are downright scary! And what keeps you safe? Speed limits, certainly. And guardrails—strong boundaries on the edges to help you stay on the narrow road. The highway department put them there, not to create jobs or spoil your view, but to keep you safe.

We need guardrails in life. I know I do. On our individual journeys we encounter hairpin turns and dangerous curves—temptations, deceit, wrong choices, making up our own rules. God's commandments give us ten "guardrails" because he knows the depths to which we can fall and how many lives can be shattered in the process. How many broken hearts, how many broken marriages, how much pain could be avoided if we stayed within these guardrail boundaries? Though bumping up against God's guardrails is inevitable, ignoring them is to do so at our own peril. But the difficult truth is, none of us makes it through life without a crash or two. Or, as is sometimes the case, without a major collision.

Scripture provides a compelling illustration of just such a collision in the story of King David's affair with Bathsheba (2 Samuel 11–12). David's untamed desire for the beautiful wife of one of his trusted officers, Uriah the Hittite, resulted in an unexpected pregnancy, a failed cover-up plan, and the eventual murder of Uriah. Displeased with David's sin, God sent the prophet Nathan to lead David into repentance. The king confessed, "I have sinned against the LORD," and Nathan replied, "The LORD has taken away your sin. You are not going to die. But because by doing this you have shown utter contempt for the LORD, the son born to you will die" (2 Samuel 12:13-14).

In the heart-wrenching lament of Psalm 51, the king of Israel poured out his confession and hope for redemption.

> *Have mercy on me, O God,*
>> *according to your unfailing love;*
> *according to your great compassion*
>> *blot out my transgressions.*
> *Wash away all my iniquity*
>> *and cleanse me from my sin. . . .*
>
> *Cleanse me with hyssop, and I will be clean;*
>> *wash me, and I will be whiter than snow. . . .*
>
> *Create in me a pure heart, O God,*
>> *and renew a steadfast spirit within me.*
> *Do not cast me from your presence*
>> *or take your Holy Spirit from me.*
> *Restore to me the joy of your salvation*
>> *and grant me a willing spirit, to sustain me.*
>>>>> *(Psalm 51:1-2, 7, 10-12)*

The burden of sin lay heavily upon the heart of this king who was so loved by God. David learned the hard way that no one crashes through God's guardrails without consequences. When we break God's law, we become stained by sin. Sin separates us from God because he is holy; and, like David, we often experience a deep sense of inadequacy when we find ourselves in God's presence.

When the prophet Isaiah found himself in the throne room of God, he cried out, "Woe to me! . . . I am ruined! For I am a man of unclean lips, and I live among a people of unclean lips, and my eyes have seen the King, the LORD Almighty" (Isaiah 6:5). And the apostle Peter, as he faced his own failings, fell to his knees in front of Jesus and cried out, "Go away from me, Lord; I am a sinful man!" (Luke 5:8).

As we enter into the presence of God, we recognize our own unworthiness and become acutely aware of our sin. We realize we'll never measure up. We can't meet God's expectations. His law is too difficult. We are too weak. With this great chasm between us and a holy God, how can we ever enter into relationship with him?

The answer to that question is *grace*.

Let's return to the Israelites in Sinai. When God spoke to them from the mountain, his timing was important. He spoke to them *after* the Exodus; after they had seen God's judgments upon Egypt, and after they experienced the Passover—saved from death by the blood of a lamb. God spoke to them after they had experienced his saving power at the Red Sea; after they escaped Egypt—guided day and night by pillars of cloud and fire—and after they had enjoyed God's mercies in the provision of manna in the wilderness and water from a rock.

Throughout these events the Israelites had experienced God's prevenient grace. Simply put, prevenient grace is grace we have not earned. It is the grace that goes before us because of the love God has for us. And it is the grace that has pursued us since the fall to sin in Eden. Because of God's great love for the Israelites—not because of anything they did—God was merciful. They had neither earned nor deserved his mercies. God hadn't forgotten them. He brought them safely out of Egypt to the foot of Mount Sinai. Then, and only then, did God give them his Law.

Grace comes before the Law. Why? Because until we experience the saving power of God in our lives, none of us can hope to keep his commandments. As human beings, we try to turn this concept around. We want to put law before grace so we can merit salvation. We look to the commandments as ten ways to earn salvation. We want to climb the holy steps of Mount Sinai on our own and earn our way to heaven with each step, scrape, and stumble. But the Bible tells us our salvation will come only after we ascend a different mountain—the mountain of Calvary—and kneel at the feet of the One who poured the blood of God's grace upon all of creation. As Paul wrote in his letter to the Ephesians:

> *For it is by grace you have been saved, through faith—and this not from yourselves, it is the gift of God—not by works, so that no one can boast. For we are God's handiwork, created in Christ Jesus to do good works, which God prepared in advance for us to do.*
>
> *(Ephesians 2:8-10)*

As the Israelites left Sinai for the Promised Land, they had the Law to keep them in a right and holy relationship with their God of thunder and fire and the grace that always went before them. But in Jesus we have the fulfillment of the law and the saving grace of the cross. For Jesus came to do what the law alone could not do—save us from the power of sin and death. Scripture illustrates this beautifully in Romans:

> *So now there is no condemnation for those who belong to Christ Jesus. And because you belong to him, the power of the life-giving Spirit has freed you from the power of sin that leads to death. The law of Moses was unable to save us because of the weakness of our sinful nature. So God did what the law could not do. He sent his own Son in a body like the bodies we sinners have. And in that body God declared an end to sin's control over us by giving his Son as a sacrifice for our sins. He did this so that the just requirement of the law would be fully satisfied for us, who no longer follow our sinful nature but instead follow the Spirit.*
>
> *(Romans 8:1-4 NLT)*

Jesus, the true Passover lamb, who shed his blood to free us from the bondage of sin and death, opened the door for us to finally ascend the sacred ground of Mount Sinai. There, we can rest—without despair—in the presence of the God of power and might. There, we can hear God speak—not in thunder, but in an intimate whisper to our hearts—*I love you. You are mine. You are the delight of my heart.* There, we are worthy of a fully restored relationship with a holy God.

One of the most famous hymns ever written is "Amazing Grace," penned by a repentant former slave trader named John Newton. His words never cease to stir my soul:

> Amazing grace! How sweet the sound
> that saved a wretch like me![2]

We are all wretches . . . but God's grace saves even the messiest of us.

Some relatives of mine lead a prison ministry in the Houston area. The inmates they serve come from all walks of life and have broken virtually every one of God's commandments. They have been convicted and sentenced for crimes such as theft, murder, rape, con-artistry, muggings, tax evasion . . . you name it, they've done it. I can hardly imagine what it would be like to hear the smack of the gavel in the courtroom as persons on trial are pronounced, "Guilty!" It must feel as though the thunder and fire of judgment has fallen upon them. In that moment freedom is no longer theirs. For many, incarceration will be lengthy; they will live within a system of stringent, unbending rules, regulations, and barriers that are designed to keep the outside world safe. What a heartbreaking reality this is for these beloved persons, created by God, who have crashed so headlong through life's guardrails.

Thankfully God's grace is present even in the harshest of circumstances. In cooperation with wardens and chaplains, the prison ministry invites inmates to attend on-site weekend retreats that are carefully and compassionately designed to introduce participants to the saving grace of the Lord Jesus Christ. The ministry team, along with prayer warriors from local church communities—and even from around the world—begin praying for the inmates and the upcoming ministry weekend long before the invitation to the inmates is extended. There is no question that the inmates who participate in a weekend are right where they are meant be. God's prevenient grace goes before them in pursuit of a personal, intimate relationship. Imagine how overwhelmed the inmates are when they learn they haven't been forgotten, that they are worthy of being loved, that their lives truly do matter.

At the end of a ministry weekend, team members and their families and friends gather with the inmates for closing ceremonies. Following a time of worship together, the inmates are invited to share their personal testimonies about the weekend. There is not a dry eye to be found in the room when these men and women weep openly as they share their experiences. One after another, the inmates tell heartbreaking stories of living lives broken by addiction, abuse, and neglect. Their most frequent admission? "I didn't know I could be loved like this."

During these weekends, many—if not all—who participate lay down their lives at the foot of the cross. Grief turns to joy as these beloved children finally understand the truth of God's word as stated by the apostle Paul, "So now there is no condemnation for those who belong to Christ Jesus" (Romans 8:1 NLT). Like the discouraged Israelites wandering in the wilderness, these inmates are taken aside for a divine appointment with their Creator. An appointment that reminds them of the truth about who they are—sons and daughters of a holy God.

We all need to experience these powerful mountaintop moments from time to time, and we don't have to go to prison to do so. Prayer and the reading of Scripture are the easiest ways we can set ourselves aside for a divine appointment with God, each and every day. These appointments will remind us of who we are and *whose* we are; they will keep us on the straight and narrow path that Jesus paved for us.

Thank God for Jesus. Thank God for sending his Son to make a way up a mountain so steep we could never climb it on our own. Thank God for providing the saving grace of the cross so that our relationships might be restored with him and with each other.

Jesus eloquently summed up this perfect plan with one statement, expanding upon the words of the words of Moses in Deuteronomy 6:5.

> *"'Love the L*ORD *your God with all your heart and with all your soul and with all your mind.'"*
> *(Matthew 22:37)*

Jesus continued:

> *"This is the first and greatest commandment. And the second is like it: 'Love your neighbor as yourself.' All the Law and the Prophets hang on these two commandments."*
> *(Matthew 22:38-40)*

All the Law hangs on these commandments—our vertical relationship with God and our horizontal relationship with each other. These two directions come together to form the shape of the cross. Reconciliation has been God's plan from the beginning.

As Moses descended from Mount Sinai with the two tablets of the Law, he carried with them the truth of God's grace. A grace that has gone before us and pursued us since the flight from Eden. A grace that will pursue us into eternity.

Through many dangers, toils, and snares,
I have already come;
'tis grace hath brought me safe thus far,
and grace will lead me home.[3]

PEAK PERSPECTIVES: NEBO

On a lonely, windswept mountaintop in Jordan, Moses and the God of Israel had their final conversation. It had been an extraordinary lifetime journey—from a floating basket in the Nile River to a pharaoh's palace, to the Sinai desert, to a forty-year trek through the wilderness. Now they found themselves together on the summit of Mount Nebo. Just the two of them.

Out of all the conversations Moses had had with God, this one likely was proving the most difficult:

> Then the LORD said to Moses, "This is the land I promised on oath to Abraham, Isaac, and Jacob when I said, 'I will give it to your descendants.' I have now allowed you to see it with your own eyes, but you will not enter the land."
> *(Deuteronomy 34:4 NLT)*

You will not enter the land . . . the Promised Land.

How disappointing it must have been for Moses, at 120 years old, to hear these words and to understand. After all, it was Moses who faithfully carried out God's command to lead the Hebrews out of Egypt. It was Moses who answered God's call to the summit of Sinai to receive and deliver the Ten Commandments to his people. It was Moses who led God's children through the wilderness in preparation for entering the land promised to him and his descendants. Yet, amidst all the years of faithful obedience, Moses had made a mistake. In a moment of frustration in the wilderness, he failed to credit God with the provision of water from a rock as he had been commanded. Instead, before the eyes of the people of Israel, he took the credit along with his brother, Aaron (Numbers 20:1-13).

It was then, apparently, that God made a change in his playbook. Someone else, a faithful, young follower of Moses—Joshua—would lead the children of Israel into the Promised Land. You and I might be tempted to think, *Whoa, that is harsh. Just one mistake and you are forbidden to complete your calling?* But if there is anything we have learned from Moses' life and his experience on Mount Sinai, we know that our God is a holy God. And, with the exception of Jesus, God shares his glory with no one.

As difficult as hearing this must have been for Moses, he had walked with God long enough to accept God's decision gracefully. God always remains faithful, even when we do not. And even though we may not fully understand, we can trust in his decisions.

> *"For my thoughts are not your thoughts,*
> *neither are your ways my ways,"*
> *declares the L*ORD.
> *"As the heavens are higher than the earth,*
> *so are my ways higher than your ways*
> *and my thoughts than your thoughts."*
> *(Isaiah 55:8-9)*

So, on the lonely Nebo mountaintop, Moses looked out on the Jordan Valley below with mixed emotions of melancholy and expectation. His long life of faithful leadership was coming to an end. Moses had prayed obediently over his people and had encouraged his successor. He reflected on all that had brought him to this place where he now stood—now, it was just him and his God. And it was at this moment that God did something remarkable. He opened his beloved prophet's eyes and gave Moses a supernatural vision of the land he would not be able to enter:

> There the LORD showed him the whole land—
> from Gilead to Dan, all of Naphtali, the territory
> of Ephraim and Manasseh, all the land of Judah as
> far as the Mediterranean Sea, the Negev and the
> whole region from the Valley of Jericho, the City
> of Palms, as far as Zoar.
> (Deuteronomy 34:1-3)

As far as the Mediterranean Sea. The panorama provided to Moses is something the naked eye cannot see from the top of Mount Nebo. As a matter of fact, only on a very clear day, when the desert dust is not stirred up, can you just barely see Jerusalem. What a gift of mercy and grace God bestowed on Moses and to all of us who join him on this mountaintop.

No matter how diligently we have dedicated our lives to following our Lord—with our triumphs and our mistakes—one day our assignments will come to an end. But the glorious lesson Mount Nebo teaches us is that *the promise of God never comes to an end*. We, too, will leave behind legacies of faithful leaders, such as Joshua, who will follow in our footsteps—accepting God's call and leading humankind into the Promised Land.

Today, at the top of Mount Nebo stands a striking Serpentine Cross sculpture. It is symbolic of the bronze serpent Moses created in the Sinai wilderness to represent the life-giving forgiveness of the children of Israel (Numbers 21:4-9). It also represents the verses in John's Gospel that say, "And as Moses lifted up the bronze snake on a pole in the wilderness, so the Son of Man must be lifted up, so that everyone who believes in him will have eternal life" (John 3:14-15 NLT).

Upon the lonely, windswept mountaintop of Nebo, we are given the merciful assurance, along with Moses, that God's promise for his children will be accomplished. And our faith in the cross of Jesus gives us the supernatural power to see far beyond the sea . . . all the way to the eternal Promised Land.

3

CARMEL: MOUNT OF DECISION

"Enter through the narrow gate. For wide is the gate and broad is the road that leads to destruction, and many enter through it. But small is the gate and narrow the road that leads to life, and only a few find it."

(Matthew 7:13-14)

Contrary to our British friends across the sea, Americans have rarely been considered a poetic people. Certainly we've had our share of those who've written verse, and much of it has been very good. But as a whole, poetry hasn't quite touched our souls as it has the British.

There is, however, one much-loved poem I suspect most of us know and can recite some, if not all, from memory—"The Road Not Taken" by American poet Robert Frost:

> Two roads diverged in a yellow wood,
> And sorry I could not travel both
> And be one traveler, long I stood
> And looked down one as far as I could
> To where it bent in the undergrowth;

Then took the other, as just as fair,
And having perhaps the better claim,
Because it was grassy and wanted wear;
Though as for that the passing there
Had worn them really about the same,

And both that morning equally lay
In leaves no step had trodden black.
Oh, I kept the first for another day!
Yet knowing how way leads on to way,
I doubted if I should ever come back.

I shall be telling this with a sigh
Somewhere ages and ages hence:
Two roads diverged in a wood, and I—
I took the one less traveled by,
And that has made all the difference.[1]

I believe this particular poem speaks to us so eloquently because it reminds us there are many roads to choose in this journey called life. Sometimes our choices seem easy and straightforward. At other times, the way forward is not so clear. But, at some point, our very lives will depend upon the choices we make.

Long after receiving God's Law at Sinai, the children of Israel were having trouble making a decision. Having settled in the Promised Land, they began in earnest to govern themselves. Leaders—or judges—acted as authorities in legal, administrative, and military matters. Although most of the judges remain largely forgotten, we remember a few because of their compelling stories in Scripture, such as Deborah, Gideon, Samson, and Samuel. Over time, though, the Israelites came to desire a king like other nations around them. "We also want a king!" became the people's cry to the prophet Samuel.

The chosen people of the kingdom of God now wanted *human* kings to lead them. God allowed them to have their kings, although I imagine God did so with a shake of the head, exclaiming, "If you insist, you may have your human kings to replace my rule, but don't say I didn't warn you." And thus began the long rule of the Israelite monarchies. Scripture records that one king after another ruled the land. The king's success, and indeed the success of the nation as a whole, depended upon the measure of the king's allegiance to God's law.

In the Book of 1 Kings, there is a striking downward spiral in the leadership and faithfulness of God's people. King after king did evil in the sight of the Lord, while only a handful of rulers actually followed God's law. And, for the most part, the children of Israel followed the allegiances of these kings—accommodating the seduction of pagan gods and false idols. Only occasionally did they follow the lead of a righteous king who was intent on leading them back to the heart of God. Faced with the questions of which road to take, and which god to follow, most of the time the Israelites chose the easy path. Israel's faithful adherence to the Mosaic covenant lost its direction, receding like waves of the evening tide. The covenant *Maker* was not at all pleased.

Decisions are not always easy to make, are they? They certainly are not easy for me. And the problem is, life's full of them. There are constant decisions to make, from the seemingly ever-present "What's for dinner?" to the more weighty "What do I want to do with my life?" With each fork in the road, we pause and ask ourselves, "Which way should I go?" I visit my favorite ice cream shop and oh, it all looks so good. The flavors are endless—chocolate macadamia, pistachio, raspberry ripple, crème brûlée, buttered pecan, sea salt caramel, coconut fudge—how can a person possibly decide? I decide to get two dips—no, maybe three—just this once. You see?

It's not easy, is it?

Imagine that you are a football coach—it's fourth down, two yards to go, five minutes left in the game, and your team is trailing by one touchdown. Do you go for it? Or do you punt? You'd love to call a time-out and tell the referee, "I want to poll the stands and let the fans vote." But you can't do that. You have to decide and live with the consequences. I think I would rather be in the ice cream shop than make *that* decision.

Whether our decisions are simple, like selecting an ice cream flavor, or more complex, like calling the final play of a championship game, I'm thankful to have the *freedom* to choose. And out of all the decisions we have the freedom to make, there is one that matters most of all—choosing whom or what we will serve. It's a decision the Israelites were having difficulty with. It's a decision an exasperated God helped them make when he called for a showdown on Mount Carmel.

Mount Carmel is located in the northern part of Israel. My wife and I visit this place every time we travel to the Holy Land, not because it's scenic (which it is), but because of what happened there some 2,800 years ago. Today a picturesque monastery sits on top of Mount Carmel. It's a dramatic location, perched high above the Mediterranean Sea. The gardens and panoramic views are stunning, but what captivates me the most is the statue of the prophet Elijah that stands at the entrance of the monastery. The statue exudes the power, zeal, and righteousness of this mighty prophet. And it's all the more gripping when you remember—*it was here! At this place. On this mountain!*—that an epic showdown took place (1 Kings 18:16-45).

Let's visit the condition of Israel leading up to this dramatic mountaintop moment. As Elijah stepped onto the stage of Israel's history, the country was in a bad way. The people had all but forgotten God. The God of their fathers—the God of Abraham, Isaac, and Jacob—seemed a distant memory. They had cast aside the law of Moses and the importance of how God dramatically rescued them from slavery in Egypt. They ceased to tell their children how God parted the Red Sea and faithfully provided manna for them in the wilderness. No longer did they kiss the soil of Israel and give thanks for the Promised Land. They took everything they had for granted. God's chosen people had followed the allegiances of an evil king into spiritual bankruptcy. They knew who God was and that Elijah was his prophet; but their commitment, loyalty, and worship waned immensely.

King Ahab was on the throne, and he was devastatingly corrupt. First Kings 16:30 tells us that "Ahab son of Omri did more evil in the eyes of the Lord than any of those before him." Even worse, Ahab was married to Jezebel, a cunning Phoenician princess from the pagan land of Sidon. Jezebel was the true power behind the throne; she had Ahab wrapped around her little finger. Her goal was to abolish the worship of the Hebrews' God and replace it with the worship of Baal, the god of her homeland. Desiring to please his wife, Ahab constructed a great temple to Baal in Israel.

Shockingly, the Bible says that in all of Israel only seven thousand people had stayed true to Yahweh (1 Kings 19:18). *Only seven thousand.* All the rest aligned themselves with the popular false god, giving only the most perfunctory nod on occasion to the God of Abraham. It looked as if Ahab and Jezebel had successfully accomplished their desire to confuse and corrupt the worship of the one true God. The Israelites had such a rich heritage; they were loved by God, chosen by God, and guided by God. How in the world could they have strayed so far away from him?

The lesson here is that *a great heritage doesn't guarantee a living faith.* The nation of Israel had a heritage steeped in the legacies of Abraham, Isaac, Jacob, and Joseph, and of their spiritual fathers Moses, Joshua, Samuel, and David. Even with this truly divine heritage, it becomes evident that you can't live off your grandfather's faith. You can't even live for long off of your father's faith. Or your mother's, for that matter.

Only seven thousand remained faithful in Israel. *How did that happen?* How did those chosen people fall into the mess of idol worship? *They slid.* They didn't cast off God and bring in Baal all at once. It was a gradual thing. It actually began a few generations earlier under the rule of Ahab's grandfather, King Jeroboam. Jeroboam wanted to ensure that the people of his Northern Kingdom (Israel) would not switch allegiances to King Rehoboam in the Southern Kingdom (Judah). So Jeroboam erected two golden calves, one at each end of the Northern Kingdom—one at Dan, the other at Bethel (1 Kings 12:25-31). Jeroboam then proclaimed "Here are your gods, Israel, who brought you up out of Egypt," quoting the words of Aaron in the story of the golden calf (1 Kings 12:28; Exodus 32:4). Jeroboam also built shrines and allowed anyone to serve as a priest, rather than choosing priests from the Levites, as God had directed. This opened wide the door of idolatry as Jeroboam's actions fed the appetites of the people. After all, the surrounding nations worshiped visible gods, idols you could see and touch; they were alluring gods who spoke to the desires of the flesh—power, money, sex, and prestige. These gods were popular with the people and didn't make so many demands, so the Israelites embraced the well-trodden path of pagan worship.

I imagine that Jeroboam knew the Israelites were weary of being different, in covenant with a God who demanded righteous and holy living. They were odd and out of step with the rest of the world. The Baals offered acceptance and pleasure. Although Jeroboam might not have intended that the people worship other gods when he brought in the two golden calves, he didn't stop the people from embracing the gods of their neighbors. It would seem Jeroboam allowed the people to make a personal choice—a private decision. Everyone could be happy; it was the best of both worlds. The faith of Israel began to slide, and they were perched on a very slippery slope.

By the time Ahab ascended the throne two generations later, the idolatry had reached such a fever pitch that worship of the one true God was barely tolerated. Worship of pagan gods was the rule in the house of Ahab; and Jezebel set out to kill the prophets and priests of the Lord God Yahweh, hunting them over the hills of Israel as if they were wild animals. The apostasy of Israel had become a landslide.

We'd be remiss if we didn't realize how easily we can slide away from our own spiritual heritages. How is it with our souls? *Have we perhaps erected a few golden calves around the edges?* I imagine most of us still hold faith in Yahweh—the true God—but what about those edges? Are we allowing idols here and there? Idols such as money, work, success, pleasure, materialism, or self? Is there compromise—tolerance of what was once not tolerated? Have the terms "universe" and "spiritual" replaced our references to God and faith? Oh, I know: our compromises seem so innocent and harmless . . . *are we sliding?*

I think most of us would honestly have to answer, "Yes, we are." That being the case, Scripture cautions us to beware, for we serve a jealous God. Remember the first commandment as given to Moses:

> *"I am the LORD your God, who brought you*
> *out of Egypt, out of the land of slavery.*
>
> *"You shall have no other gods before me."*
> *(Exodus 20:2-3)*

Turning away from God is serious business, as the children of Israel were about to find out. Except for the mere seven thousand, the people largely abandoned their faith under the rule of Ahab and Jezebel. So God sent a drought. For three years he withheld blessing from heaven and it rained not a drop. Without rain, the people could not grow crops. Israel was hungry and miserable.

Then, at the darkest hour, when all hope seemed lost, God acted. Without warning and without introduction, the prophet Elijah burst upon the scene. For three years he had been hiding in the desert, waiting for the right moment to proclaim God's truth to Ahab and the nation. The showdown was about to begin.

Before we continue, let's consider this Elijah for a moment. Who exactly was he? We don't know much about this mysterious prophet, but the Bible tells us he was a Tishbite, "from Tishbe in Gilead" (1 Kings 17:1 ESV). Elijah was a follower of Israel's God, and his name means "Yahweh is God"—a significant name in a time when Baal worship threatened to extinguish the worship of Yahweh in Israel.

One thing we do know about Elijah is that his conviction and courage cause him to stand out as one of the great heroes of the Hebrew people. Why is this prophet so revered? It's because at a critical moment in Israel's history he stood firm for monotheism. When all the cultural tides were against him, Elijah fought against syncretism, summoning the courage to defy the king of Israel and challenge the false prophets of Baal.

Not only was Elijah revered in the Old Testament, but his influence can be seen in the New Testament as well. After his mysterious disappearance from earthly life in a whirlwind (2 Kings 2:1-17), the prophet Malachi proclaimed God's promise that Elijah would return again:

> *"See, I will send the prophet Elijah to you before*
> *that great and dreadful day of the Lord comes."*
> *(Malachi 4:5)*

Later, Jesus referred to Malachi's prophecy when discussing John the Baptist:

"For all the Prophets and the Law prophesied until John. And if you are willing to accept it, he is the Elijah who was to come."
(Matthew 11:13-14)

And, in a magnificent mountaintop moment on Mount Tabor, Elijah and Moses appeared together in glory during the transfiguration of Jesus.

After six days Jesus took with him Peter, James and John the brother of James, and led them up a high mountain by themselves. There he was transfigured before them. His face shone like the sun, and his clothes became as white as the light. Just then there appeared before them Moses and Elijah, talking with Jesus.
(Matthew 17:1-3)

It is no wonder that when God set the stage for a showdown against the prophets of Baal on Mount Carmel, he sent Elijah.

Maybe it's my Texas roots, but I love to watch a good, old-fashioned western movie about the wild, wild west that is set in a hot, dry, desert town. A gang of evil outlaws rides into town to challenge the authority of the good sheriff and his deputies. You know how the storyline goes: The challenge is accepted, and a duel is set for high noon. Terrified townspeople watch, as they hide behind storefront windows. The clocktower chimes slowly toward twelve. With hands on their holsters, the opponents face each other, and the sheriff's silver star badge is glinting sharply in the sunlight as he takes his place alongside his deputies. Just a few moments after the clock strikes twelve, the bloody battle is over, and one stands victorious—the one wearing the shining silver star. It's a classic showdown not unlike the one that occurred nearly 2,800 years ago on a mountain in Israel.

Out of the hot, dry, desert appeared a fearless prophet of God named Elijah. Elijah squared off with King Ahab and boldly stated his purpose. Let's pick up the story in 1 Kings 18.

> *"And now you tell me to go to my master and say, 'Elijah is here.' He will kill me!"*
>
> *Elijah said, "As the LORD Almighty lives, whom I serve, I will surely present myself to Ahab today."*
>
> *So Obadiah went to meet Ahab and told him, and Ahab went to meet Elijah. When he saw Elijah, he said to him, "Is that you, you troubler of Israel?"*
>
> *"I have not made trouble for Israel," Elijah replied. "But you and your father's family have. You have abandoned the LORD's commands and have followed the Baals."*
>
> (1 Kings 18:14-18)

Elijah then issued his challenge to Ahab:

> *"Now summon the people from all over Israel to meet me on Mount Carmel. And bring the four hundred and fifty prophets of Baal and the four hundred prophets of Asherah, who eat at Jezebel's table."*
>
> (1 Kings 18:19)

This guilty king now knew that he and his queen had no choice but to answer this defiant prophet's demand. The challenge was accepted. The location was selected. The opponents? *Baal* and God.

So Ahab sent word throughout all Israel and assembled the prophets on Mount Carmel. Elijah went before the people and said, "How long will you waver between two opinions? If the Lᴏʀᴅ is God, follow him; but if Baal is God, follow him."

But the people said nothing.

(1 Kings 18:20-21)

But the people said nothing. The people stood on Mount Carmel facing a divine fork in the road, and they couldn't make a decision. Should they take the wider, more comfortable, more popularly traveled road or the narrower, less traveled road being followed by only a faithful few? They just couldn't decide.

Have you ever heard of the term *mugwump*? Not to be confused with "muggle" from *Harry Potter* notoriety, the term mugwump was fashioned in 1884 during an election to describe one who is a "fence-sitter"—with their "mug," or face, on one side, and their "wump" (a play on "rump") on the other.[2] A frustrated Elijah stood before a literal crowd of mugwumps on the mountain as he cried out, *"How long will you waver between two opinions?"* (verse 21).

Elijah's question echoes across the centuries. Every soul must answer it. How long will you waver and hesitate? We're not talking about ice cream here. We're not deciding a football play. We're called to choose our spiritual destiny. God brings us all up to Mount Carmel; and there, he demands a decision. And if we are truly honest, I imagine even the best of us can place ourselves in the crowd of mugwumps on Mount Carmel, even though, time and time again, we have been reminded in Scripture about the dangers of serving two gods at the same time.

James 1 warns, "A double minded man is unstable in all his ways" (James 1:8 KJV). And in Revelation 3:15-20 Jesus makes it very clear in his message to the church in Laodicea that a luke-warm, neutral, accommodating, compromising body is repulsive to the Lord and damaging to his purpose.

But, like the Israelites, we tend to want the best of both worlds. We hang onto our "temple in Jerusalem," yet we allow our golden calves to muddy the spiritual waters of our faith in the one true God. Jesus' reminder in Matthew 22:37 to "love the Lord your God with all your heart and with all your soul and with all your mind" is but a distant whisper. Jesus knew that our false gods would be worthless and impotent, incapable of saving us.

Elijah knew that too. And so we stand with Israel on the top of Mount Carmel, witnessing together the great prophet as he orchestrates a mighty showdown.

> *Then Elijah said to them, "I am the only one of the LORD's prophets left, but Baal has four hundred and fifty prophets. Get two bulls for us. Let Baal's prophets choose one for themselves, and let them cut it into pieces and put it on the wood but not set fire to it. I will prepare the other bull and put it on the wood but not set fire to it. Then you call on the name of your god, and I will call on the name of the LORD. The god who answers by fire—he is God."*

> *Then all the people said, "What you say is good."*

> *Elijah said to the prophets of Baal, "Choose one of the bulls and prepare it first, since there are so many of you. Call on the name of your god, but do not light the fire." So they took the bull given them and prepared it.*

> *Then they called on the name of Baal from morning till noon. "Baal, answer us!" they shouted.*

But there was no response; no one answered. And they danced around the altar they had made.

At noon Elijah began to taunt them. "Shout louder!" he said. "Surely he is a god! Perhaps he is deep in thought, or busy, or traveling. Maybe he is sleeping and must be awakened." So they shouted louder and slashed themselves with swords and spears, as was their custom, until their blood flowed. Midday passed, and they continued their frantic prophesying until the time for the evening sacrifice. But there was no response, no one answered, no one paid attention.

Then Elijah said to all the people, "Come here to me." They came to him, and he repaired the altar of the LORD, which had been torn down. Elijah took twelve stones, one for each of the tribes descended from Jacob, to whom the word of the LORD had come, saying, "Your name shall be Israel." With the stones he built an altar in the name of the LORD, and he dug a trench around it large enough to hold two seahs of seed. He arranged the wood, cut the bull into pieces and laid it on the wood. Then he said to them, "Fill four large jars with water and pour it on the offering and on the wood."

"Do it again," he said, and they did it again.

"Do it a third time," he ordered, and they did it the third time. The water ran down around the altar and even filled the trench.

At the time of sacrifice, the prophet Elijah stepped forward and prayed: "LORD, the God of Abraham,

*Isaac and Israel, let it be known today that you are God in Israel and that I am your servant and have done all these things at your command. Answer me, L*ORD*, answer me, so these people will know that you, L*ORD*, are God, and that you are turning their hearts back again."*

*Then the fire of the L*ORD *fell and burned up the sacrifice, the wood, the stones and the soil, and also licked up the water in the trench.*

*When all the people saw this, they fell prostrate and cried, "The L*ORD*—he is God! The L*ORD*—he is God!"*

(1 Kings 18:22-39)

*When all the people saw this, they fell prostrate and cried, "The L*ORD*—he is God! The L*ORD*—he is God!"* Just like that, the bloody showdown was over. The people of Israel no longer sat on the fence. Their decision was clear. In a spectacular moment of power and glory, the God of Abraham, Isaac, and Jacob rained down his fire upon the altar on Mount Carmel, reigniting the flames of faith and belief in the hearts of his chosen people.

Wouldn't it be nice if the story ended at that point? But there is a postscript, as so often there is in Holy Scripture. The Bible does not gloss over the humanity of its champions. It does not present them as Marvel comic book superheroes. Rather, we are presented with real people who have real emotions and weaknesses.

For Elijah, the battle continued after Mount Carmel, and it was not against outward foes. This battle was waged within himself. As we turn the page from 1 Kings 18 to 1 Kings 19, we see a completely different side of this presumably fearless prophet of

God. Now, we come face-to-face with a fragile man who was fearful and insecure.

When King Ahab told Queen Jezebel everything Elijah had done, and how he had killed all the prophets with the sword, Jezebel sent a messenger to Elijah with her threat: "The gods will get you for this and I'll get even with you! By this time tomorrow you'll be as dead as any one of those prophets" (1 Kings 19:2 MSG).

How did Elijah, this great prophet of God, respond? Like you and I probably would—he ran for his life.

> When Elijah saw how things were, he ran for dear life to Beersheba, far in the south of Judah. He left his young servant there and then went on into the desert another day's journey. He came to a lone broom bush and collapsed in its shade, wanting in the worst way to be done with it all—to just die: "Enough of this, GOD! Take my life—I'm ready to join my ancestors in the grave!" Exhausted, he fell asleep under the lone broom bush.
>
> *(1 Kings 19:3-5 MSG)*

After God's impressive defeat of Baal on Mount Carmel, you would think Elijah would be celebrating; but instead *Elijah slid into despair*. It is human nature for emotions to overcome us at times, especially when we are tired. That is when we can most easily become discouraged; when all options seem bleak . . . when we feel abandoned.

Was Elijah afraid? Absolutely. It must have been terrifying to be hunted by the angry queen. And he felt all alone. This was not the first time Elijah felt this way. Back on Mount Carmel, as he addressed the gathered Israelites, Elijah said to them, "I am the only one of the LORD's prophets left, but Baal has four hundred and fifty prophets" (1 Kings 18:22).

Indeed, as Elijah hid from Jezebel in the desert, he thought he was the only one left; but he was to learn otherwise. After seeing that Elijah was fed and rested, God told him about the faithful remnant—the seven thousand of his fellow countrymen—who were also in hiding. Not one of them had bowed a knee to Baal.

We, too, can feel as though we are alone in this world. We might even become discouraged; we are living in a society that increasingly does not share our Judeo-Christian values and at times seems even hostile to people of faith. What Elijah discovered was that the LORD God Yahweh had more faithful followers than he had been aware—followers who shared Elijah's belief and values. There is strength in numbers, and for Elijah this must have been a source of relief and encouragement. This great prophet of God found his footing once again and went on to anoint future kings of Israel. He also prophesied the demise of the house of Ahab and Jezebel.

We need to remember this lesson today. How easy it is for us to become downcast and fall into pessimism. Sometimes I am guilty of sliding into the "Elijah complex" way of thinking—feeling overwhelmed by the larger society, which does not seem to share my commitment to godly principles. And when this happens, God faithfully has a way of awakening me, of opening my eyes to clearer understanding by reminding me: *There are others like you. Those who care. Those who believe. Those who want justice and goodness. Those who remain faithful. You are not alone.*

Have you ever felt this way? Alone and overwhelmed, thinking, *I'm the only one who cares. It's all on me?*

In times like these we need to remember God is not sitting on the sidelines, nor is God outnumbered or outmatched. We have more brothers and sisters who share our faith and our commitment than we are aware. Sometimes God snaps us out of our pessimism though Holy Scripture. As we read our Bibles, God's word opens our minds and we gain a clearer perspective. We remember that God is in charge. At other times God sends friends to encourage us, friends who remind us that God sent his light into this world and that darkness has not overcome it.

Back in the 1800s the debate over slavery tore our nation apart. Concerned men and women spoke passionately against it, calling our country to repentance. One of the most famous was a man named Frederick Douglass. After escaping from slavery in Maryland, Douglass became a national leader of the abolitionist movement. He was a frequent speaker in abolition rallies across the North and Midwest; he also wrote an autobiography, which became a best-selling book quickly, both in America and Europe.

In 1847 Frederick Douglass was the featured speaker at an antislavery meeting at Faneuil Hall in Boston. Being emotionally exhausted, a discouraged Douglass had begun to despair. A note of pessimism worked its way into his address. He feared terribly for the future of the African American people, and he questioned if slavery could ever be abolished in a peaceful manner. His fear and despair mounted; and as the suggestion of insurrection entered his address, a woman rose up and shouted from the gallery, "Frederick, is God dead?" It was the voice of the famous African American Sojourner Truth. A legend in her own right, she and Frederick Douglass both belonged to the same African Methodist Episcopal Zion Church in New York City, and both of them crossed the nation preaching for social justice.[3]

Sojourner Truth's piercing question lifted Douglass's spirits and renewed his hope. It reminded him that through the power of the Holy Spirit, the will of God would prevail.

> *"'Not by might nor by power, but by my Spirit,'*
> *says the LORD Almighty."*
> (Zechariah 4:6)

Like Frederick Douglass—and Elijah—life circumstances can cause us to become despondent, downcast, and desperate. We need to remember that even great people of faith have moments of weakness. Even those we admire most are still human with real emotions and real insecurities. This does not diminish them; it only means they are human.

Like Sojourner Truth—and Elijah—we need to remind the world that God is still on the throne and is still in charge. Even though *we* may grow weary, God will never grow tired or weary (Isaiah 40:28). Sojourner Truth's question, *"Is God dead?"* ignited the fire of hope in Frederick Douglass and the abolitionist movement in 1847.

Thousands of years before Sojourner's cry, the fire of God poured down upon Mount Carmel in response to the cry of Elijah, "Answer me, LORD, answer me, so these people will know that you, LORD, are God" (1 Kings 18:37). It was a fire that would reignite the flame of belief in Israel.

Elijah's battle on Mount Carmel and the battle over slavery in the 1800s were difficult roads to travel for all involved; they were fraught with danger, fear, indecision, and disappointment. We also encounter difficulties on the roads we walk today. But as we listen to the cries from Scripture and history, our way is made clear. For as the psalmist reminds us,

> *Your word is a lamp for my feet,*
> *a light on my path.*

(Psalm 119:105)

From the burning bush to the pillars of fire in the wilderness; from the fiery cloud on Sinai to the flames of Elijah's altar on Mount Carmel; the holy fire of God has served as a mighty beacon, lighting the way for those with the courage and faith to choose the narrow road. Today God shines his mighty light on the road we all must travel—the road that leads to Calvary. On *that* mountain, a final showdown took place upon a cross. And the One left standing victorious is the One who was born under a shining star—the One who loves you and desperately wants to hear your voice proclaim, *"The Lord—he is God! The Lord—he is God!"*

PEAK PERSPECTIVES: MASADA

On the rocky mountaintop of Carmel, a dramatic decision was made during a mighty showdown. Eight hundred and fifty prophets of Baal met their demise as Elijah and the people of Israel proclaimed their loyalty to the one true God.

Nearly nine centuries later, another rocky mountaintop was the setting of yet another showdown—and another decision. The name of this mountain is Masada.[4]

Masada rises to a height of 1,500 feet above the Dead Sea. It is the location of the desert fortress and extravagant palace complex that was constructed by Herod the Great between 37 and 31 BC. Its haunting story is as tragic as it is mysterious, and the story has served as the inspiration for several movies and books.

Jewish historian Flavius Josephus chronicled the intriguing story of this mountain in his writings *The Wars of the Jews*.[5] The land of Israel became a province of the Roman Empire in 40 BC. Herod was appointed king of Judea; and several years after his death in 4 BC, Judea fell under the direct administration of Rome. New Testament Scripture provides many accounts of this period in Jewish history during the lifetimes of Jesus and the apostles.

As the years went by, the Jewish people became more and more displeased with living life under the cruelty of Roman occupation, and in AD 66 the Great Revolt of the Jews broke out against the Romans. Masada had been confiscated as a fortress by the Romans at the time of Herod's death, and during the Revolt, it was overtaken by an elite group of Jewish Zealots. They used this self-sustaining fortress as their base of operations; and from there, the Zealots continued to lead their insurgency against the Romans. They encouraged all Jews to join them in wresting back their land and way of life.

But it was not to be. In AD 70 Jerusalem and the Temple were destroyed by the Roman army. Hundreds of thousands of Jews perished or were sold into slavery. We can only imagine the terror and grief the people of Israel experienced, and we can understand the tears of Jesus as he wept over his beloved city of Jerusalem, for his words certainly foreshadowed these events:

> *"For the days will come upon you, when your enemies will set up a barricade around you and surround you and hem you in on every side and tear you down to the ground, you and your children within you. And they will not leave one stone upon another in you, because you did not know the time of your visitation."*
>
> *(Luke 19:43-44 ESV)*

The surviving rebels of the siege of Jerusalem escaped to Masada with their families—a group totaling 960 men, women, and children. These resolute Jews would hold out on this desert mountaintop fortress for three years, while the Roman army slowly built a ramp up the side of the mountain to reach them.

Whenever possible, the rebels continued their attempts to thwart the plans of the enemy below. As brave as these fighters were, we can imagine the concern they must have experienced on a daily basis, with the certainty of torture, slavery, and death inching its way up the mountainside. What would they do when the Roman army reached the top? Would they fight? What about the women and children? They would undoubtedly be carried off to Rome and suffer unspeakable horrors.

So, as Josephus writes in his account, the Jews at Masada made a heartbreaking decision. On the first day of Passover, in April of AD 73, it became clear a breach of the fortress was imminent. The Jews proceeded to set fire to the fortress and then killed each other—every man, woman, and child—and the last remaining rebel took his own life. They left their food supply intact so the Romans would understand starvation was not the cause of their deaths. Their decision was one of resolve to live as servants of no one except the one true God, and in death they would find the freedom they sought.

When the conquering Roman army entered Masada, they expected to put an end to this troublesome rebel contingent and celebrate a hard-fought victory. But this victory would be a hollow one, steeped in mystery—and silence. When they stepped onto Masada, they were met with a pile of bodies. *What on earth had happened here?*

Several days later, the Romans would learn the truth when two women and five children emerged from their hiding place in one of the fortresses' deep underground water cisterns. They were the only survivors and would tell the tragic and moving story of Masada to all who would listen, including Josephus.

As with many ancient stories, there is much speculation about what truly transpired in those final moments of the Jewish revolt on Masada. But one thing stands out: the Jewish people made a decision—one that would inspire and capture the hearts of future generations of the people of Israel.

The decisions of Mount Carmel and Masada were forged on spiritually charged battlegrounds. On Carmel, the prophets of Baal died because they would not serve the one true God of Israel.

On Masada, the last group of Jewish holdouts died because they would serve only the one true God of Israel. To this day, whenever the jets of the Israeli Defense Force fly over Masada, they tip their wings in tribute to the heroism of their faithful compatriots. The story of Masada is truly haunting and tragic. It's a remarkable story of a people who were radically committed to their God.

4

BEATITUDES: MOUNT OF BLESSINGS

When Jesus heard that John had been put in prison, he withdrew to Galilee. Leaving Nazareth, he went and lived in Capernaum, which was by the lake . . . to fulfill what was said through the prophet Isaiah . . .

> *"the people living in darkness*
> *have seen a great light;*
> *on those living in the land of the shadow of death*
> *a light has dawned."*

From that time on Jesus began to preach, "Repent, for the kingdom of heaven has come near."
(Matthew 4:12-17)

Our mountaintop journey of discovery together began with a side trip. If you remember, it was to visit Mount Rushmore in

South Dakota. There we imagined which of the great biblical leaders might be featured on the face of the mountain in an "Old Testament version" of Rushmore. Abraham, Moses, and Elijah were among our selections—I'd say we chose well indeed.

As we begin our exploration of New Testament mountaintop moments, I'd like to indulge in one more side trip, this time a little further west of Rushmore—to the Continental Divide, also known as the Great Divide.

Bev and I made this same side trip with our children many years ago. We drove across the Continental Divide on a road trip vacation through the Rocky Mountains in Colorado. Of course, we stopped to take pictures. Before the kids started scrambling around, trying to find a nonexistent black line drawn on the ground, we explained to them that the Continental Divide was the demarcation of watershed in our part of the world. Beginning in the Bering Strait of Alaska, this Divide runs through the entirety of the North and South American continents and ends in the Strait of Magellan at the tip of South America. All rainwater and snowmelt on one side of the Divide eventually flows to the Pacific Ocean, while all the rainwater and snowmelt on the other side of the Divide flows into the Atlantic and Arctic Oceans and the Gulf of Mexico.[1] This little side trip proved to be a great living history lesson for our family.

Now, as we continue our biblical mountaintop journey, we step from the Old Testament into the New Testament. Here, we're about to cross another great divide, not in geography, but in theology. This great divide is Jesus.

We join Jesus early in his ministry, as chronicled in the Gospel of Matthew, chapters 4-7. Following his time of temptation in the desert, Jesus burst onto the scene with his opening sermon at the synagogue in Nazareth. Most of his early ministry occurred around the Sea of Galilee, a freshwater body of water that is fed by the Jordan River—truly a life-giving source for Israel. Jesus traveled throughout this region, teaching in synagogues, healing the sick, and proclaiming, "Repent, for the kingdom of heaven has come near" (Matthew 4:17). The Bible records that the people "listened to him with delight" (Mark 12:37) and followed him in droves. His preaching was not like the other rabbis. He taught as one who had authority, and the people were amazed. On one occasion the crowd grew so large that Jesus had to get into a boat and make it his pulpit. People pressed forward to the water's edge, as they hung onto Jesus' every word, while he sat teaching from the boat (Luke 5:1-3).

Jesus was constantly in demand, but he managed to slip away occasionally and climb to a quiet place on a hill rising high above Galilee to spend time in reflection and prayer with his heavenly Father, away from the crowds. Upon his descent, however, he would discover new crowds waiting on the hillside, who were eager to hear more of his teachings and receive the gift of his healings. So Jesus would sit under the shade of the olive trees and teach them. Jesus' disciple Matthew describes these hillside ministry moments in a compilation of teachings called the Sermon on the Mount.

One of my favorite places in the Holy Land is the Church of the Beatitudes. It is a beautiful place, located on a steep hill, or bluff, overlooking the Sea of Galilee. It is built on the traditional site believed to be where Jesus delivered the Sermon on the Mount. No one knows if this is the precise location, but the site has been venerated by Christian pilgrims since at least the fourth century. And the current church sits near the ruins of a small Byzantine-era church, which dates back to that time. Archaeologists have recovered part of the original Byzantine mosaic floor, which is now on display in Capernaum.

Whether this is the actual location of the Sermon on the Mount or not, you can't help but feel a connection there to Jesus and his disciples. Upon a visit to the Church of Beatitudes, the late Fr. Jerome Murphy-O'Connor[2] observed that from its vantage point high above Galilee, pilgrims have a bird's-eye view of Jesus' life and ministry.

Truly, the entire area feels like a sanctuary—a holy place. Among the many visiting pilgrims from around the world, Catholic monks and priests are seen frequently on the church grounds and on the hillside praying and worshiping—their melodies of chant rising and falling with the wind as it moves among the olive trees. It's hauntingly beautiful . . . one might say, even otherworldly.

As Jesus began to deliver his Sermon on the Mount, his listeners—disciples, admirers, and scoffers—were about to have an otherworldly experience. In the person of Jesus Christ, a new world had planted itself in their midst—a world they would discover to be far different from their own—a world Jesus insisted would be their future. This world was the kingdom of heaven—the same kingdom that Jesus proclaimed to have "*come near.*" As the crowds pressed in around him, he opened his sermon with a curious series of blessings, which we know as the Beatitudes.

> *Now when Jesus saw the crowds, he went up on a mountainside and sat down. His disciples came to him, and he began to teach them.*
>
> *He said:*
>
> *"Blessed are the poor in spirit,*
> *   for theirs is the kingdom of heaven.*
> *Blessed are those who mourn,*
> *   for they will be comforted.*

Blessed are the meek,
for they will inherit the earth.
Blessed are those who hunger and thirst for
righteousness,
for they will be filled.
Blessed are the merciful,
for they will be shown mercy.
Blessed are the pure in heart,
for they will see God.
Blessed are the peacemakers,
for they will be called children of God.
Blessed are those who are persecuted be-
cause of righteousness,
for theirs is the kingdom of heaven.

"Blessed are you when people insult you, perse-
cute you and falsely say all kinds of evil against
you because of me. Rejoice and be glad, because
great is your reward in heaven, for in the same way
they persecuted the prophets who were before
you."

(Matthew 5:1-12)

Join me now for a moment on the hillside among the listening crowd. Our gazes shift from Jesus to the people standing around us. We are incredulous. What is the rabbi saying? What does he mean that we should be blessed—or happy—to be poor, mournful, meek, hungry, and persecuted? Our world certainly doesn't teach that. We are to strive for abundance, happiness, strength, satisfaction, success—what?

Jesus continues, speaking in plain language so we are sure to understand. With regard to faith, he speaks about being the salt of the earth, full of vitality and flavor, and warns of becoming taste-less. Your faith will season the lives of others as you continue to be strong and mature in your faith. He speaks of being the light of the world that is set high on a hill for people to see. He tells us not to hide our light—our talents, abilities, and faith—from the world (Matthew 5:13-15). Instead, he says, "Let your light shine before others, that they may see your good deeds and glorify your Father in heaven" (verse 16).

As Jesus continues, his teachings become more difficult, as steep as this hillside that has become his pulpit. Although the elevation of the Mount of Beatitudes is not known, we do know it is not easily climbed. The standards Jesus is laying out before us are simply too high for us to imagine, much less achieve. Consider some of his next words:

> *"You have heard that it was said to the people long ago, 'You shall not murder, and anyone who murders will be subject to judgment.' But I tell you that anyone who is angry with a brother or sister will be subject to judgment."*
>
> *(Matthew 5:21-22)*

> *"You have heard that it was said, 'You shall not commit adultery.' But I tell you that anyone who looks at a woman lustfully has already committed adultery with her in his heart."*
>
> *(Matthew 5:27-28)*

> *"It has been said, 'Anyone who divorces his wife must give her a certificate of divorce.' But I tell you that anyone who divorces his wife, except for sexual immorality, makes her the victim of adul-tery, and anyone who marries a divorced woman commits adultery."*
>
> *(Matthew 5:31-32)*

"You have heard that it was said, 'Eye for eye, and tooth for tooth.' But I tell you, do not resist an evil person. If anyone slaps you on the right cheek, turn to them the other cheek also. And if anyone wants to sue you and take your shirt, hand over your coat as well."

(Matthew 5:38-40)

"You have heard that it was said, 'Love your neighbor and hate your enemy.' But I tell you, love your enemies and pray for those who persecute you, that you may be children of your Father in heaven."

(Matthew 5:43-45)

"Be perfect, therefore, as your heavenly Father is perfect."

(Matthew 5:48)

By now, we are dizzy from the heights we are expected to climb. Even our thoughts and emotions can lead us down the wrong path? We are to love our enemies . . . even pray for them? We are expected to be perfect, like God? What is this rabbi doing? He is completely turning our world upside down with his teachings.

Actually, what Jesus was doing was turning the world of his listeners right-side up. In presenting a heavenly perspective of what life on earth should look like, Jesus provided a preview of what's ahead when "your kingdom come" from the Lord's Prayer is finally answered (Matthew 6:10). Jesus drew a dividing line on the Mount of Beatitudes between the world of man and the kingdom of heaven, and he invited his listeners to make a choice. In truth, he had drawn a chasm, a chasm that could only be bridged by belief and faith in the yet-to-come.

Two thousand years ago, on a silent night in Bethlehem, a king was born that would change the world forever. Jesus' own words tell us that he stepped from the throne of heaven where he shared the glory face-to-face with God the Father before the universe was created (John 17:5). The son of God put on human flesh, arrived through a miraculous birth, and was called Immanuel—"God with us" (Matthew 1:23). The glorious invasion of heaven on earth had begun, and Jesus was at the center of it.

People paid attention. Something was different. This was no ordinary prophet. Most of the earliest followers of Christ, like those he preached to in Galilee and on the Mount of Beatitudes, were Jews who believed in his authority and teaching. Ultimately they came to believe in his divine Kingship.

Jesus told the truth about what God expected of Kingdom people. He told people what they needed to hear, not just what they wanted to hear. These days, I'm afraid, we place so much emphasis on God's acceptance and forgiveness and grace that we're prone to neglect the other side of the gospel; and that is, God cares about righteous living. Not just in our beliefs but in our behavior.

During the days of Jesus' ministry, the Jewish people were still living under the Mosaic covenant as given to them at Sinai and shaped by hundreds of laws. Their law primarily spoke to the outward expression of their faith—the way they worshiped; how and when they worked; how they treated their own kind; and how they treated those they considered to be unsuitable or unclean. Hebrew males, from the time of Abraham, bore an outward sign of living under covenant with God in the form of circumcision. But Jesus came to fulfill the law—to usher in a new covenant which embodied the spirit of the law. This covenant required an inward expression of faith—a circumcision of the heart.

As Jesus taught beneath the olive trees on the Mount of Beatitudes, he drew aside the curtain of the heavenly realm and provided his listeners with a glimpse into this unseen Kingdom. With his delivery of the Beatitudes—the blessings—he extended both a promise and an invitation. First, he praised his disciples, who had already embraced the Kingdom and were living lives of poverty, mercy, and even persecution in service to it. Jesus promised that the eternal blessings of the Kingdom were already theirs: "Theirs is the kingdom of heaven" (Matthew 5:3). To the surrounding crowds, Jesus extended an invitation—if you will live this way, and follow me as these disciples have, the blessings of the Kingdom will be yours.

If you had been one of those on the hillside listening, whether as an admirer, questioner, or scoffer, might you have turned your ear to listen a little more carefully? Might your heart have started beating a little faster as you heard the promises given to these disciples, these followers of Jesus? Might a spark of hope have caused your spirit to jump as you wondered if maybe you could also have these eternal blessings of a heavenly kingdom? Might you have also wondered, *How do I get from the world I live in—to that?*

Following the Beatitudes, Jesus presented six contrasts between the traditional teachings of the Torah and the new teachings of the Kingdom of Heaven. Six times, beginning with murder and ending with love for your enemies, he opened with the statement, "You have heard that it was said" and quoted the teaching of the Jewish law. And six times he exclaimed, "But I tell you. . . ." The explanation that followed showed how the old way is not enough, and it reveals the spirit of the law.

Jesus offered a more exacting standard of righteousness and challenged people to a new way of living—Kingdom living. He knew his teaching ran counter to the world his listeners knew and lived in, so he gave them assurances that would strengthen them if they dared to step out and follow him. Jesus knew that faith is a journey that takes a lifetime—a lifetime of trusting, learning, stumbling, getting back up, and trying again. It's a journey that has no visible path, so he provided a source of internal navigation for Kingdom people to follow.

Jesus assured his listeners that God knows their needs and hears their prayers. He knew, on a very personal level, that prayer is a powerful way to stay connected to the Kingdom—it supplies and sustains the faith of believers. So Jesus provided instruction on praying with simplicity and suggested a prayer his listeners could employ in their daily lives.

> *"And when you pray, do not be like the hypocrites, for they love to pray standing in the synagogues and on the street corners to be seen by others. Truly I tell you, they have received their reward in full. But when you pray, go into your room, close the door and pray to your Father, who is unseen. Then your Father, who sees what is done in secret, will reward you. And when you pray, do not keep on babbling like pagans, for they think they will be heard because of their many words. Do not be like them, for your Father knows what you need before you ask him.*

> *"This, then, is how you should pray:*

> *"'Our Father in heaven,*
> *hallowed be your name,*
> *your kingdom come,*
> *your will be done,*
> *   on earth as it is in heaven.*
> *Give us today our daily bread.*
> *And forgive us our debts,*
> *   as we also have forgiven our debtors.*
> *And lead us not into temptation,*
> *but deliver us from the evil one.'"*
> (Matthew 6:5-13)

Jesus also advocated leaving anxiety and worry in the hands of a loving God who cares deeply for the needs of his children:

"Which of you, if your son asks for bread, will give him a stone? Or if he asks for a fish, will give him a snake? If you, then, though you are evil, know how to give good gifts to your children, how much more will your Father in heaven give good gifts to those who ask him!"

(Matthew 7:9-11)

With his delivery of the Sermon on the Mount, Jesus Christ presented the first-century people of Israel with an astonishing look at a new world, a new way of life, and a mighty choice to make. Which world would they belong to? The question remains the same for us today. Will we choose to continue to belong to a world of selfishness, persecution, retaliation, and death? Or will we choose to belong to a world of mercy, compassion, holiness, and eternal life? We are invited to live otherworldly lives in a desperately fallen world with a relentless calling.[3]

Those who choose to follow a Kingdom life with Jesus will experience the blessing of seeing the workings of the realm of God, which this world does not yet see. In his book, *The Longing for Home*, renowned author and theologian Frederick Buechner offers a compelling description of how Jesus views our world: "For all its horrors, the world is not ultimately a horror show because, as Jesus tells us, the world has the Kingdom buried in it like a treasure buried in a field."[4] Buechner goes on to tell the story of a 1913 fiftieth-anniversary reenactment of Pickett's Charge, the final assault of the Battle of Gettysburg. Carried out by aged Union and Confederate veterans, the old men took up their positions and then started marching toward each other. And then Buechner says something extraordinary happened. "As the old men among the rocks began to rush down at the old men coming across the field, a great cry went up, only instead of doing battle as they had half a century earlier, this time they threw their arms around each other. They embraced each other and openly wept."[5]

Truly, on a fifty-year-old battlefield, these men had discovered the buried Kingdom treasure. They were more alike in their humanity than they were different. The years had quietly replaced the passion to fight on the battlefield with the passion to love one another. *This is what they, and all of us, were created to do.*

Loving others is the very essence of Jesus' teaching on the Mount of Beatitudes. He considered it to be so important that later in his ministry he issued a new commandment: "Love each other as I have loved you" (John 15:12). This commandment was not just for his early followers; it was for everyone, because his kingdom is for everyone. The Bible records one of the earliest prophecies about the coming kingdom of Jesus in the Book of Genesis, when God made a promise to Abraham:

> The LORD had said to Abram, "Go from your
> country, your people and your father's household
> to the land I will show you.
>
> "I will make you into a great nation,
>   and I will bless you;
> I will make your name great,
>   and you will be a blessing.
> I will bless those who bless you,
>   and whoever curses you I will curse;
> and all peoples on earth
>   will be blessed through you."
> *(Genesis 12:1-3)*

Jesus the Christ, from the line of Abraham, brought with him the Kingdom that would bless all the nations of the earth. After his resurrection, Jesus issued another commandment, known as the Great Commission:

> "All authority in heaven and on earth has been
> given to me. Therefore go and make disciples of all

*nations, baptizing them in the name of the Father
and of the Son and of the Holy Spirit, and teaching
them to obey everything I have commanded you.
And surely I am with you always, to the very end
of the age."*

(Matthew 28:18-20)

Very clearly, all people are invited to follow Jesus into a new way of living. But there is a caveat. Jesus' teachings reveal that the way into the Kingdom is challenging. The gate is narrow. A change of heart is necessary and so is childlike faith. The requirements are as difficult as the Mount of Beatitudes is steep. And Jesus knew that all who choose to follow him will stumble and fall along the way.

I'm reminded of the incredible test of endurance that comes to my town every year—the Ironman Triathlon. The triathlon consists of a 2.4-mile (3.9-kilometer) swim, a 112-mile (180-kilometer) bike ride, and a 26.2-mile (42.1-kilometer) run. Participants are allowed seventeen hours to complete all three legs of the race. I can't even imagine the lifetime of training it takes to participate in such a journey of physical—and mental—endurance. I'm certain there are injuries and setbacks along the way; but these athletes keep at it, training for their goal to be the best they can be. It's an emotional experience to watch the athletes approach and cross the finish line. They are determined, and they are exhausted. Sometimes I think the hardest steps are their last steps—the ones they need to take with the finish line in sight. They are almost there. And some of them literally collapse on the ground from exhaustion with the finish line just yards away, unable to continue. But then something wonderful happens. To the detriment of their own timed race result, fellow athletes will stop, lift the fallen ones from the ground, and carry them across the finish line.

This is what Kingdom living is all about, and this is what our Messiah does for us as we follow him. The curtain he drew aside on a hillside at the beginning of his ministry was the same curtain he pulled down upon a cross on Calvary. We can depend upon his saving grace to pick us up when we stumble and to carry us to the finish line when we are unable to complete the journey on our own.

Even today, Jesus continues to be the great divide. He has made clear that the only way to enter the kingdom of heaven is through him. So he still stands on that dividing line he drew on the Mount of Beatitudes. His voice still calls to us from that holy sanctuary on the hill . . . his words rising and falling with the wind that moves through the olive trees. They are some of the most beautiful words ever spoken. They are one of the greatest blessings ever offered to humankind. *Follow me.*

PEAK PERSPECTIVES: OLIVET

Follow me. Jesus' invitation to join him in a new way of living—Kingdom living—was one that would prove both wonderful and challenging to his listeners on the Mount of Beatitudes. It was an invitation he would extend throughout his ministry, along with the reassuring promise to prepare the way for those willing to accept.

As Jesus stood at the top of Mount Olivet on his final day of earthly ministry, preparations for his followers were well underway. Olivet, or the Mount of Olives, is a mountain ridge that sits just outside of the Old City area of Jerusalem. Named for the olive trees that covered its slopes, Olivet figured significantly into the events of Jesus' ministry and into the preparations he had been making.

Bethany, on the mountain's eastern slope, was the home of Jesus' friends—Mary, Martha, and Lazarus; and, also, Simon the Leper. It is where Jesus wept over the city as he made his triumphant Palm Sunday ride into Jerusalem. At the base of the mountain sits the lovely garden of Gethsemane. It was here, in this quiet place among the olive trees, that Jesus prayed and was betrayed. Scripture records that Bethany is the place where Jesus ascended into heaven. And Scripture also tells us "his feet shall stand on the Mount of Olives that lies before Jerusalem" (Zechariah 14:4 ESV) on the day of the Lord's second coming.

With every step Jesus took along the paths and places of this holy mountain, he was preparing a way for Jews and Gentiles alike to follow him into the kingdom of heaven. He fellowshipped. He healed. He raised the dead. And he taught.

On the night of his last supper with his disciples, Jesus said to them, "Where I am going, you cannot follow now, but you will follow later" (John 13:36). The disciples were confused, so Jesus used a story to help them understand:

> *"Do not let your hearts be troubled. You believe in God; believe also in me. My Father's house has many rooms; if that were not so, would I have told you that I am going there to prepare a place for you? And if I go and prepare a place for you, I will come back and take you to be with me that you also may be where I am. You know the way to the place where I am going."*
>
> *(John 14:1-6)*

As Jesus often did, he spoke in the language of the culture—a language his listeners would understand. With this story, he gave his disciples a telling insight into what he was doing and what was coming.

In Jesus' time people often lived in a large family compound, called an *insula*.[6] Extended families lived together in a series of rooms constructed around a common open courtyard. According to tradition, when a young man wished to marry a young woman, he would present to her a cup of wine. If she drank from the cup, it meant she accepted his proposal. At this point the young man would return to his own family's insula, where he and his father would set to work, adding a new room onto the family compound. The material they used was stone, so the construction process was a painstaking labor of love—involving hands, feet, blood, sweat, and, likely, a few tears. Once the room was complete the young man would return to the young woman's insula, marry her, and take his bride home to live with him and his extended family.

In the days and weeks that followed, the disciples would understand the message of this story. Jesus was indeed preparing a place for them in his kingdom. His hands and feet were nailed to a cross. Blood and sweat mingled with his tears as he suffered and died—in the ultimate labor of love. And with his glorious resurrection, Jesus opened wide an entryway for all who wished to follow him.

But there were more preparations to be made—this time from the heavenly throne room. In the final moments of Jesus' earthly ministry, he promised that a helper—the Holy Spirit—would come to be with the disciples in his absence. Then "when he had led them out to the vicinity of Bethany, he lifted up his hands and blessed them. While he was blessing them, he left them and was taken up into heaven" (Luke 24:50-51). Acts 1:10-11 says, "They were looking intently up into the sky as he was going, when suddenly two men dressed in white stood beside them. 'Men of Galilee,' they said, 'why do you stand here looking into the sky? This same Jesus, who has been taken from you into heaven, will come back in the same way you have seen him go into heaven.'"

Luke also tells us the disciples left the Mount of Olives and returned to Jerusalem "with great joy" (Luke 24:52). It's no wonder they were joyful—even the angels knew the truth the disciples now understood. It's a truth in which we can rejoice as well.

We have heard our dear Savior's call, *Follow me*, from the Mount of Beatitudes. And we have followed the way he prepared for us, all the way to the Mount of Olives. Now, with the disciples and all of the saints, we wait with great anticipation. The Father and the Son are busy preparing a place for us. And when all the preparations are complete, our Lord Jesus Christ will return to Olivet to bring us all to live with him—in the glorious insula of the King!

5

TABOR: MOUNT OF TRANSFIGURATION

All your works praise you, Lᴏʀᴅ;
your faithful people extol you.
They tell of the glory of your kingdom
and speak of your might,
so that all people may know of your mighty acts
and the glorious splendor of your kingdom.
(Psalm 145:10-12)

Throughout the years, filmmakers have taken us on many exciting and thought-provoking adventures. I suppose most of us have a list of our favorite movies. My list includes classics such as *Casablanca*, *Lawrence of Arabia*, and Alfred Hitchcock's *Vertigo*. A more recent movie that I enjoyed was a comedy-drama film titled *The Bucket List*,[1] starring Jack Nicholson and Morgan Freeman, one of the top ten movies of the year in 2007. The plot follows two terminally ill men on a road trip with a wish list of things to do before they "kick the bucket."

Although their lives are worlds apart—one is a blue-collar worker and the other a billionaire businessman—they find a common bond in their desire to live what is left of life to the fullest.

And they do. Between bouts of sickness the two men travel the globe, crossing off their heart's desires. Their creative adventures take them to exotic locations such as India, China, Africa, Egypt, and Nepal. But in an endearing twist, the men discover that the rekindling of devotion for a spouse, the restoration of an estranged relationship with a daughter, and the chance to kiss a little grand-daughter's cheek for the first time far outweigh the satisfaction of their worldly adventures. As their lives draw to a close, their lists are complete. Although their suffering has been great, their buckets are overflowing . . . with love.

Have you ever considered what you might put on your own "bucket list"? Would you want to view Paris at night from the top of the Eiffel Tower? Or hike the spectacular North Rim of the Grand Canyon? Or experience a sunrise from the top of one of Hawaii's volcanoes? Maybe you'd like to cheer on magnificent Thorough-breds as they run for the roses at the Kentucky Derby. Or satisfy your need for speed at the Indianapolis Motor Speedway's Indy 500. Or see who earns the honor of wearing the coveted green jacket of the Masters Tournament at the Augusta National Golf Club in Georgia. (I recently crossed that one off my own bucket list.)

Perhaps your list might be more relational in nature—to walk your daughter down the aisle at her wedding, hold your first grand-child in your arms, or celebrate a fiftieth wedding anniversary with the one who has forever captured your heart.

In a sense, as we have journeyed together throughout these mountaintops of Egypt and Israel, we have been exploring a spir-itual bucket list—a list scripted by heaven itself. We've immersed ourselves in the lives and adventures of Abraham, Isaac, Moses, and Elijah. And as we approach our next mountain, Jesus is about to take us on another extraordinary adventure. It begins at the very gates of hell.

Twenty five miles from Jesus' primary ministry region of Galilee sits Caesarea Philippi. Now known as the Golan Heights near the Syrian border, it is a lush area located near the foot of Mount Hermon. In Old Testament times, this northeastern area of Israel became a center for pagan worship. As you will recall from our journey to Mount Carmel, pagan worship surreptitiously slid into Israelite religious practice after King Jeroboam erected altars at Dan in the north and Bethel in the south.

Caesarea Philippi, located near the ancient city of Dan, became entrenched in pagan worship; and in Jesus' day it had become the religious center for worship of the Greek god Pan. Half man and half goat, Pan was a frightful god of nature and fertility who dwelt in mammoth, bottomless caves that were believed to be entrances to the underworld. To appease and entice Pan, worshipers engaged in detestable acts of worship, including sexual immorality.[2] This type of pagan worship was widespread in the Mediterranean region at the time of Jesus.

The god known as Pan to the Greeks was known to the Romans as Faunus. Recent archaeological excavations have unearthed a huge bronze mask of Pan and the structural ruins of a Roman gateway, believed to be part of a sanctuary or temple dedicated to Pan, located just outside Hippos-Sussita, a city overlooking the eastern shore of the Sea of Galilee. Like Caesarea Philippi, this location is consistent with sites of Pan worship, held outside of the city in forested areas and caves due to the nature of worshipers' ecstatic rituals.

When it has been safe to travel to the Golan Heights, Bev and I have taken many groups to see the area of Caesarea Philippi. The hike up through the lush foliage at the base of Mount Hermon to the Grotto of Pan is beautiful. Streams flow from deep under-ground springs that supply the great Jordan River; and as a clearing opens up ahead, you are met with a stunning and eerie sight: a dark, yawning entrance to a mammoth cave just behind the ruins of a temple to Pan. According to pagan legend, those who stand there behold the very gates of hell.

As Jesus neared the end of his earthly ministry, he took his disciples on a long and curious side trip—a retreat to the Grotto of Pan at Caesarea Philippi. The disciples must have been absolutely shocked. This was an unholy place; it was a "sin" city in every sense of the word. This visit certainly was *not* on their bucket lists. What in the world was Jesus doing by bringing them to this detestable place? Matthew tells us that as Jesus stood near the pagan temple, he posed a question to his disciples:

> *When Jesus came to the region of Caesarea Philippi, he asked his disciples, "Who do people say the Son of Man is?"*
>
> *They replied, "Some say John the Baptist; others say Elijah; and still others, Jeremiah or one of the prophets."*
>
> *"But what about you?" he asked. "Who do you say I am?"*
>
> *Simon Peter answered, "You are the Messiah, the Son of the living God."*
>
> *Jesus replied, "Blessed are you, Simon son of Jonah, for this was not revealed to you by flesh and blood, but by my Father in heaven. And I tell you that you are Peter, and on this rock I will build my church, and the gates of Hades will not over-come it. I will give you the keys of the kingdom of*

heaven; whatever you bind on earth will be bound in heaven, and whatever you loose on earth will be loosed in heaven."

(Matthew 16:13-19)

Who do you say I am? This was a critical teaching moment for Jesus. The cross was looming over him, and he knew the time had come for his disciples to fully understand the message he had been preaching. For three years they had been walking with him in a traveling seminary—hearing his teachings and observing his healings. But soon they would be on their own without him, and Jesus wanted to make certain they were prepared, confident, and equipped.

Simon Peter's bold response, *"You are the Messiah, the Son of the living God,"* transformed their little gathering with the light of truth. Upon Peter's admission, Jesus gave his disciples a look at the future of their ministry: *"On this rock I will build my church, and the gates of Hades will not overcome it."* As Jesus stood before the looming, dark cave, he knew his disciples faced a lifetime of literally facing down death and darkness with the good news of the gospel—soon to be revealed in his suffering, death, and resurrection. Upon the rock of Peter's faith, Jesus was commissioning his disciples to be the force of life against death and to establish the church everywhere they could.

Jesus' teaching at Caesarea Philippi must have seemed as deep and formidable as the ominous cave to his disciples, and it became more so as he revealed the truth, for the first time, about what was coming next.

> *From that time on Jesus began to explain to his disciples that he must go to Jerusalem and suffer many things at the hands of the elders, the chief priests and the teachers of the law, and that he must be killed and on the third day be raised to life.*

*Peter took him aside and began to rebuke him.
"Never, Lord!" he said. "This shall never happen to
you!"*

(Matthew 16:21-22)

Jesus' disciples, his beloved and faithful followers, were deeply distressed. Suffering was not to be the path of their Messiah. *No!* Their Messiah was to come in glory and rule in triumph. They had not understood the nature of the kingdom of heaven. They wanted a crown; Jesus offered a cross. His was a gospel of service and sacrifice.

"Whoever wants to be my disciple," Jesus told his disciples, "must deny themselves and take up their cross and follow me. For whoever wants to save their life will lose it, but whoever loses their life for me will find it" (Matthew 16:24-25). What the disciples failed to understand was that glory would come only after suffering.

Six days passed . . . days of disappointment and confusion. The disciples just couldn't wrap their minds around the cross—that Jesus would have to die. So their beloved rabbi planned one more side trip before they headed for Jerusalem. He took his inner circle, Peter, James, and John, to a high place for prayer. This place was Mount Tabor, a small mountain rising abruptly from the surrounding flat plains, eleven miles west of the Sea of Galilee. What follows is one of the most unusual and breathtaking experiences recorded in the Gospel accounts; recorded not just once, but three times, in the Gospels of Matthew, Mark, and Luke.

*After six days Jesus took with him Peter, James
and John the brother of James, and led them up
a high mountain by themselves. There he was
transfigured before them. His face shone like the
sun, and his clothes became as white as the light.*

Just then there appeared before them Moses and Elijah, talking with Jesus.

Peter said to Jesus, "Lord, it is good for us to be here. If you wish, I will put up three shelters—one for you, one for Moses and one for Elijah."

While he was still speaking, a bright cloud covered them, and a voice from the cloud said, "This is my Son, whom I love; with him I am well pleased. Listen to him!"

When the disciples heard this, they fell facedown to the ground, terrified. But Jesus came and touched them. "Get up," he said. "Don't be afraid." When they looked up, they saw no one except Jesus.

As they were coming down the mountain, Jesus instructed them, "Don't tell anyone what you have seen, until the Son of Man has been raised from the dead."

(Matthew 17:1-9)

What a remarkable mountaintop moment. Let's pitch a tent (build a shelter), as Peter suggested, and stay here for just a bit to let this sink in. First of all, why did Jesus take valuable time away from his ministry to climb this mountain? Weren't there hungry people to be fed? sick to be healed? lessons to be taught? hurting people to be helped? Why did Jesus take this time away from his mission? After all, time was running out!

Why? *Because his disciples needed it.* They needed to know that all he had been teaching them about himself was true. They needed a glimpse of the victorious Christ. Verse 2 tells us, "*There he was transfigured before them. His face shone like the sun, and his clothes became as white as the light.*"

This was a transforming event for these three disciples. In a spectacular moment, they saw Jesus in his glory—the glory he had with God before the world began (John 17:5). Finally, the disciples began to comprehend the enormity of who Jesus was. Peter's first admission at Caesarea Philippi that Jesus was the Messiah, the Son of the living God, was an admission based on faith. Now, on Mount Tabor, Peter, James, and John were eyewitnesses to a stunning truth. Jesus was indeed the Messiah, the One sent by God to redeem Israel and this fallen world.

The transfiguration of Jesus gave this inner circle of beloved followers *confidence*—assurance they were following the right person. It also gave them *courage*. Jesus knew he was calling his disciples to a difficult life. With the exception of Judas Iscariot, who perished after his betrayal of Jesus (Matthew 27:3-5), the apostles would remain faithful to the life Jesus had called them. Matthew and John went on to write two of the four Gospels. John also penned the Book of Revelation. Peter, "the rock," became the leader of the early church. The itinerant ministries of the early disciples carried the good news of the gospel to places near and far, including Jerusalem, India, Armenia, Greece, Turkey, Spain, Syria, Africa, Egypt, and Iraq.[3]

The apostles' faithfulness would not be without hardship and sacrifice. Many of them experienced imprisonment. And although there is much speculation about how the apostles died, we do know the facts about some of them. James, son of Zebedee, died at the hand of King Herod Agrippa in AD 44. Acts 12:1-2 says, "It was about this time that King Herod arrested some who belonged to the church, intending to persecute them. He had James, the brother of John, put to death with the sword." The Roman writer Tertullian indicated that Peter and Paul were martyred in Rome under the rule of the emperor Nero.[4] John may have been the only apostle to have died of old age. He was sentenced to a life in exile on the remote island of Patmos, where he eventually died.

Jesus knew all too well that as his disciples brought the light of God's kingdom into the world, the darkness would push back. Their confidence in the gospel would keep these dedicated followers committed to the task entrusted to them. Losing their lives was not something they would have looked forward to, but they could face the coming trials because they had seen Jesus in his glorified state. It was something they would never forget.

Just before Peter was martyred in AD 67, he wrote a letter to the church as a reminder of the truth of Christianity, as opposed to the heresies of false teachers. In it he states,

> *For we did not follow cleverly devised stories when we told you about the coming of our Lord Jesus Christ in power, but we were eyewitnesses of his majesty. He received honor and glory from God the Father when the voice came to him from the Majestic Glory, saying, "This is my Son, whom I love; with him I am well pleased." We ourselves heard this voice that came from heaven when we were with him on the sacred mountain.*
>
> *(2 Peter 1:16-18)*

And John wrote this about Jesus: "The Word became flesh and made his dwelling among us. We have seen his glory, the glory of the one and only Son, who came from the Father, full of grace and truth" (John 1:14).

These beloved disciples carried with them the revelation of Jesus' transfiguration throughout their lives, and the written word of their testimony has encouraged believers throughout the ages.

Now don't pack up your tent yet . . . there is more to explore here. The appearance of two of the greatest prophets and messianic forerunners of the Old Testament—*Moses and Elijah*—

occurred in this miraculous moment. As they appeared, they began talking with Jesus. I can only imagine what went through the minds of Peter, James, and John as they huddled together, watching this incredible mountaintop meeting. Their beloved rabbi was speaking with the twin pillars of Jewish religious history—the two great leaders of the old covenant—men whom they had studied and read about in the Torah.

Moses was the Law-giver and the one in whom God established a covenant relationship with the nation of Israel. His words foreshadowed the coming of a Savior when he told the Israelites, "The LORD your God will raise up for you a prophet like me from among you, from your fellow Israelites. You must listen to him" (Deuteronomy 18:15).

Elijah was the restorer—the thundering prophet of truth—who called people back to the law and the covenant. After Elijah had been taken to heaven, God promised the people, "Behold, I will send you Elijah the prophet before the great and awesome day of the LORD comes" (Malachi 4:5 ESV). This prophecy was first fulfilled in the life and death of John the Baptist. In Jesus' own words, "Elijah comes and will restore all things. But I tell you, Elijah has already come, and they did not recognize him, but have done to him everything they wished. In the same way the Son of Man is going to suffer at their hands" (Matthew 17:11-12).

So what were Moses and Elijah saying to Jesus? Of the three Gospel accounts of the transfiguration, only Luke gives us information about what the three were discussing in this meeting on the mountain: "Two men, Moses and Elijah, appeared in glorious splendor, talking with Jesus. They spoke about his departure, which he was about to bring to fulfillment at Jerusalem" (Luke 9:30-31).

Moses and Elijah were discussing Jesus' *departure*. In Greek, this word is *exodos*. The first Moses, who led God's people out of slavery into freedom, was speaking about the next exodus with the *new Moses*—Jesus. Jesus was the bringer of the new covenant—the one who would lead God's people from death to life, from sin to redemption. Elijah and Moses were present to help prepare Jesus for his final exodus and return to glory.

In the transfiguration moment, Moses and Elijah, the greatest of the law-givers and the greatest of the prophets of the Old Testament, were united. They knew the one they were speaking with was the one who fulfilled both the law and the prophecies of the past. The one who had been foretold. The one who would suffer and die in Jerusalem.

By this time, Peter, James, and John were nearly speechless with amazement and terror. Peter blurted out to Jesus, "Lord, it is good for us to be here. If you wish, I will put up three shelters—one for you, one for Moses and one for Elijah" (Matthew 17:4). Why he said this, no one is sure. He may well have just wanted to prolong the experience, to have everyone hang out there on the mountaintop for a while together, something many of us do when we have intensely meaningful moments. We don't want our experience to be over—we want to savor it before rejoining the "real world." But one thing is certain: because of their dazzling appearance, described as "glorious splendor" in Luke 9:30, Peter may have assumed Jesus, Moses, and Elijah were equally divine. So God himself stepped in to set the record straight.[5]

> *While he [Peter] was still speaking, a bright cloud covered them, and a voice from the cloud said, "This is my Son, whom I love; with him I am well pleased. Listen to him!"*
>
> *When the disciples heard this, they fell facedown to the ground, terrified. But Jesus came and touched them. "Get up," he said. "Don't be afraid."*

> *When they looked up, they saw no one except Jesus.*
>
> (Matthew 17:5-8)

This is my Son, whom I love; with him I am well pleased. Listen to him! In that instant, the exclusive deity of Jesus was confirmed. God himself answered the question Jesus put to his disciples at Caesarea Philippi, *"Who do you say I am?"* (Matthew 16:15). God proclaimed, *"This is my Son."* God also professed his love for Jesus, *whom I love.* "For God so loved the world that he gave his one and only Son" (John 3:16). How painful that love had to be—a sacrificial love that bore a ministry of suffering for the redemption of humanity. Finally, God said, *"Listen to him!"* The disciples also knew these words from Moses' prophecy about Jesus as recorded in Deuteronomy 18:15: *"You must listen to him."* With this final statement, God made it clear—do not ignore Jesus' words. Do not doubt his truth. Trust him. Believe him; for there is no other way to salvation, except through him.

With their own ears, Peter, James, and John heard and understood the truth as spoken by the very voice of God. Jesus was truly the Son of God, the Messiah. Moses and Elijah were gloriously resurrected prophets—men who had lived righteous lives in covenant with God. Not only were these men the forerunners of Christ, they also served as *foretellers* for the disciples and all who are believers. Their dazzling appearance foretold of the glory we also will receive when we are resurrected in Christ.

As we pack up our tents and head down the mountain with Jesus, Peter, James, and John, we know we are changed forever by what we have seen and heard. Danish philosopher, theologian, and author Soren Kierkegaard, once wrote, "What really counts in life is that at some time one has seen something, felt something, which is so great, so matchless, that everything else is nothing by comparison, that even if he forgot everything he would never forget this."[6] I suspect this is an apt description of what the disciples must have felt after their experience on Mount Tabor, as well as for us, as our eyes and hearts are opened by this amazing account.

As Jesus descended the mountain, he told his disciples to tell no one about their experience until after he was raised from the dead (Matthew 17:9). That must have been a very difficult secret to keep. They had just witnessed something incredible. Supernatural. Divine. They had actually seen how the glory of God looked! They knew well the story of Moses' encounter with God's glory at Mount Sinai when he received the Ten Commandments.

> *When Moses came down from Mount Sinai with the two tablets of the covenant law in his hands, he was not aware that his face was radiant because he had spoken with the LORD. When Aaron and all the Israelites saw Moses, his face was radiant, and they were afraid to come near him. But Moses called to them; so Aaron and all the leaders of the community came back to him, and he spoke to them. Afterward all the Israelites came near him, and he gave them all the commands the LORD had given him on Mount Sinai.*
>
> *When Moses finished speaking to them, he put a veil over his face. But whenever he entered the LORD's presence to speak with him, he removed the veil until he came out.*
>
> *(Exodus 34:29-34)*

When Moses met with God, his face became radiant. God's glory was so dazzling that it encompassed everything around it—even Moses. Moses *reflected* God's glory. And now, the disciples had seen this phenomenon with their own eyes! Jesus' face shone like the sun, *radiating* God's glory, because of who he is. He *is* God. Jesus didn't reflect the glory, he *is* the glory!

We might be tempted to think this amazing transformation to Jesus' appearance first occurred on the mountain when he started to glow—when his face shone like the sun. But the true transformation of Jesus happened long before that . . . at the moment of his birth. God—the glorious, magnificent ruler of all creation—became an ordinary, tiny human baby who lay in a manger.

In order to rescue and redeem a suffering world, God had to become a part of that world. Our world. He had to become one of us. And so he stepped from his throne *and gave up his glory*. This babe in a manger was God incarnate. *Immanuel*—"God with us."

To imagine what it cost Jesus to give up his life on the cross is difficult. But I don't think we can even come close to imagining what it cost Jesus to give up his power and majesty and take the form of a man. His sacrifice truly was twofold. Jesus sacrificed the magnificent throne of heaven to become the prophesied suffering servant—the Messiah—and sacrificed his life to redeem our fallen world.

The account of Jesus' transfiguration on Mount Tabor is a rather brief story as Scripture goes, but the fact that it was recorded in three of the Gospels speaks to its lasting importance in the lives of the disciples and their ministry, and in our own lives today.

In the days following the retreat at Caesarea Philippi, the disciples were distressed and confused by Jesus' revelation that he would soon take them to Jerusalem, where he would suffer, be put to death, and be resurrected. They had learned that though their ministry would go on without him, life would be difficult. Six days after they stood in front of the gates of hell at Caesarea Philippi, they stood on Mount Tabor and watched as Jesus was miraculously revealed as God's own Son and radiated the glory he had in heaven before he came to earth—the same glory to which he would return when his ministry was fulfilled.

What an incredible moment and what an incredible gift. In the span of a week, Jesus led his beloved disciples from the gates of hell to the threshold of heaven. In these transformational teaching moments, they witnessed the reality of our fallen world—sin, suffering, and death—and the truth of the victory and glory that were to come. Jesus' promise that the gates of Hades would not overcome his church was true.

The disciples had seen something so great, so matchless, that they would never forget it. It gave them confidence. It gave them courage. It gave them assurance that in Jesus Christ, glory will follow suffering. They began to understand that the crown they expected *would* come, but only after the cross.

If I were to make out a spiritual bucket list, this experience would have to be right at the top. How many of us would love to actually witness, as the disciples did, this preview of heaven that Jesus provided on Mount Tabor!

Thankfully, we have the witness of Scripture to remind us of this miraculous event, enabling us to "believe without seeing" (John 20:29 NLT). What a great comfort it is to know that as followers of the risen Christ, no matter what we and those we love suffer here in this fallen world, we can look forward with assurance to the glory of heaven.

The gates of hell continue to release torrents of suffering into this world—both physical and emotional. I have observed that those who suffer the most gracefully are those who model the self-less, sacrificial love of Jesus.

One of the most moving examples of this kind of sacrificial living is the dedication and service of our armed forces and first responders—those who are willing to step into the trenches of death and destruction and are willing to lay down their own lives so that others may live.

Perhaps some of you have seen the extraordinary and critically acclaimed film, *Hacksaw Ridge*,[7] which debuted in 2016. The film is based on the World War II experiences of Desmond Doss, an American combat medic and Seventh-day Adventist Christian, whose refusal to carry or use a weapon stemmed from his conviction to his religious beliefs.

Doss carried deep within him the confidence and courage of his faith and had an unwavering belief in the sanctity of human life and God's commandment, "Thou shalt not kill" from Exodus 20:13 (KJV). As you can easily imagine, this refusal to bear arms bewildered his fellow soldiers and commanding officers and opened him up to frequent, and often severe, judgment, including beatings.

That ridicule changed entirely during the Battle of Okinawa. Doss's unit was tasked with securing a formidable escarpment nicknamed "Hacksaw Ridge." Multiple offensives to take control left heavy casualties on both sides; and, at one point, the Americans lost control of the ridge to the Japanese forces. Doss became aware that several of his fellow soldiers were left injured and dying on the field of battle. So he returned to save them, armed only with his medic's kit and the small Bible he carried with him—a gift from his wife.

The movie is spell-binding. Single-handedly, and against all odds, Doss dodged unrelenting grenade and firing attacks, carrying his fallen squad-mates to the edge of the ridge and lowering them to the ground with ropes. It was exhausting physically; and with each rescue, Doss prayed for the strength to save at least one more.

As the number of rescued wounded grew at the bottom of the ridge, so grew the admiration and inspiration of Doss's fellow soldiers and commanding officers. This heroic effort inspired the American forces. Fresh troops were brought in, and the tide of the battle turned to an American victory.

In the final hours of the battle for Hacksaw Ridge, Doss was wounded by a grenade, which he survived. He was later awarded the Medal of Honor for service above and beyond the call of duty during the Battle of Okinawa.

This true story is a remarkable example of a remarkable faith. This young soldier stood at the gates of hell—amid the horrors of war, death, and suffering—relying on his faith in a loving God who reigns victorious over all things. The path he had chosen was not an easy one. He suffered persecution. He suffered injury. But he believed in Jesus and in the promise that one day all things will be made new. He believed that when his suffering was over, he would experience for himself the glory of a resurrected life in Christ. And in his willingness to lay down his life for others, many lives were saved. Lives who would be given the chance to know Jesus.

His was the life of a disciple, one who follows the example of Jesus while living life here on earth. One who risks everything for the redemption of others. One who "believes without seeing" the miraculous promise given on Mount Tabor—the promise of the glory that follows the cross.

As the disciples followed Jesus on what would be his final trip to Jerusalem, they were prepared. When Jesus returned to glory, these twelve would become the great apostles of our Christian faith and build the church of Jesus Christ upon the rock of Peter's confession . . . *"You are the Messiah, the Son of the living God"* (Matthew 16:16). Though their suffering would be great, their ministry overflowed, with love.

Today, as the church, we are beneficiaries of that great sacrificial love. So we come together regularly to confess our statement of faith—a faith that was lived, breathed, and witnessed by the apostles of Jesus Christ.

The Apostles' Creed, Traditional Version

I believe in God the Father Almighty,
    maker of heaven and earth;

And in Jesus Christ his only Son our Lord:
    who was conceived by the Holy Spirit,
        born of the Virgin Mary,
        suffered under Pontius Pilate,
        was crucified, dead, and buried;
    the third day he rose from the dead;
    he ascended into heaven,
        and sitteth at the right hand of God
    the Father Almighty;
    from thence he shall come to judge the
quick and the dead.

I believe in the Holy Spirit,
    the holy catholic[8] church,
    the communion of saints,
    the forgiveness of sins,
    the resurrection of the body,
    and the life everlasting. Amen.[9]

PEAK PERSPECTIVES: CALVARY

In a miraculous moment on top of Mount Tabor, God drew aside the veil of heaven to provide Peter, James, and John with a startling and surreal revelation. Their dear friend and rabbi was revealed in all his glory as the Son of the living God.

> *And he was transfigured before them, and his clothes became radiant, intensely white, as no one on earth could bleach them. And there appeared to them Elijah with Moses, and they were talking with Jesus. And Peter said to Jesus, "Rabbi, it is good that we are here. Let us make three tents, one for you and one for Moses and one for Elijah." For he did not know what to say, for they were terrified.*
>
> *(Mark 9:2b-6 ESV)*

It's no wonder the disciples were afraid. They had literally just experienced a glimpse behind the veil into the heavenly realm! The veil between heaven and the realm of humanity exists for a reason—to keep heaven's mysteries hidden until their appointed time. Jesus commanded his disciples to tell no one what they had witnessed on Mount Tabor "until the Son of Man had risen from the dead" (Mark 9:9 ESV). For he knew that soon a great mystery would be revealed in an earth-shattering moment atop a different mountain. On this mountain, Calvary, another veil would be completely torn in two.

Calvary is a rocky, barren hill located just outside of Jerusalem's Damascus Gate. It is a place of death—also known as Golgotha— the place of the skull. With the revelation of heaven still fresh in their minds, the disciples now found themselves on Calvary and in the depths of despair. Their teacher and friend was dying on a cross. *How in the world could they reconcile these two dramatically different events? It didn't make sense.* But what God did next provided the reconciliation they sought so desperately.

> *And Jesus cried out again with a loud voice and yielded up his spirit.*
>
> *And behold, the curtain of the temple was torn in two, from top to bottom. And the earth shook, and the rocks were split. The tombs also were opened. . . . When the centurion and those who were with him, keeping watch over Jesus, saw the earthquake and what took place, they were filled with awe and said, "Truly this was the Son of God!"*
> *(Matthew 27:50-52, 54 ESV)*

The veil of the Temple—the *parokheth*—was known in the tradition of the people of Israel as "the tunic of God."[10] It served as a barrier to the Holy of Holies, where God resided with the ark of the covenant. No one could enter this area except the high priest, and then only on Yom Kippur—the Day of Atonement. On this most holy day of the year, the high priest would enter the Holy of Holies through the veil to offer a blood sacrifice for the sins of the people.

With Jesus' last breath on the cross, the God of creation tore his tunic from top to bottom. In this divine act of anguish and love, the veil of the Temple was torn in two, and so was the body of God's only Son. Jesus became the everlasting atonement for the sins of the world. The way into God's presence had been opened for all. The Way *is* Jesus.

On Mount Tabor, Jesus was transfigured, and "his clothes became shining, exceedingly white, like snow" (Mark 9:3 NKJV). The moment Jesus died on Mount Calvary, his blood took away the stain of our sins, making them whiter than snow.

And on Calvary, the reconciliation the disciples sought was provided in Jesus, the Great High Priest—revealed in glory and eternal sacrifice.

> *Therefore, since we have a great high priest who has ascended into heaven, Jesus the Son of God, let us hold firmly to the faith we profess. For we do not have a high priest who is unable to empathize with our weaknesses, but we have one who has been tempted in every way, just as we are—yet he did not sin. Let us then approach God's throne of grace with confidence, so that we may receive mercy and find grace to help us in our time of need.*
>
> *(Hebrews 4:14-16)*

6

ZION: MOUNT OF GOD'S PRESENCE

"Do not come any closer," God said. "Take off your sandals, for the place where you are standing is holy ground." Then he said, "I am the God of your father, the God of Abraham, the God of Isaac and the God of Jacob."

(Exodus 3:5-6)

Had we applied this command from ancient scripture throughout our mountaintop journey, our bare feet would most surely be tired, worn, and dusty by now. Together we have traced the sacred paths of Abraham and Isaac, Moses, Elijah, and the followers and disciples of Jesus—paths that led them, and us, into the very presence of a holy God. We have witnessed sacrificial love on Mount Moriah, covenant on Sinai, revival on Carmel, divine blessing on Beatitudes, and triumphant glory on Tabor. And if you're like me, your knees must also be scraped and sore from bowing under the sheer wonder and weight of heaven's tideless sea of love and provision.

Today, as we set out on our final journey, we turn our faces to the east and join our voices with the children of Israel in joyful songs of praise. We are making a pilgrimage to the holiest place on earth—the mount of God's presence. We are heading to *Zion*.

> *For the Lord has chosen Zion,*
> *he has desired it for his dwelling, saying,*
> *"This is my resting place for ever and ever;*
> *here I will sit enthroned, for I have desired it."*
> (Psalm 132:13-14)

Have there been times in your life when you have felt especially close to God? Or have there been special places where the presence of God overwhelmed you—places where you just wanted to sit and soak in God's very presence? Bev and I have experienced just such a time and a place. It happened during our college days at Asbury College in Wilmore, Kentucky. On February 3, 1970, during the regularly scheduled 10 a.m. chapel service, heaven opened without warning, and God visited us in a powerful way.

I'd like to share Bev's personal recollection of this remarkable event, and of the days and weeks that followed, for it truly is an apt description of what we, and many others, experienced when God showed up on campus.

> The Asbury revival was like nothing else I've ever experienced. There's never a February 3rd that passes that I don't remember what happened on that day in 1970.
>
> We had our regularly-scheduled chapel—it was on a Tuesday. The women's ensemble was scheduled to sing that morning, and I was in that group. We sang "When I Survey the Wondrous Cross" just before the sermon. The academic dean was supposed to speak but told us he

didn't feel led to speak. So he gave a testimony and then invited anyone who wanted to share their personal faith experiences to come to the microphone. Students began to share, and the Holy Spirit was so strong in that room—no one wanted to leave. The dean announced that classes were cancelled for the day, and everyone stayed to pray and share, confess their sins, and receive healing. It continued all day and into the night.

The next morning it was still going on and continued around the clock for at least a week. We would go to grab some food and sleep and return to soak in the atmosphere of the Holy Spirit working so powerfully in all of our lives. We would pray and share how the Lord was leading us, pray for each other and encourage one another. Before long, it wasn't just the students who were confessing and sharing. Professors, people in the community—even our local pastor—came to share what was happening in their lives and how the Holy Spirit was convicting them. They also confessed their sins, and reconciled with people in the community.

Media began to arrive to do stories for their television programs and newspapers, so word really traveled quickly then. People called our school to ask for teams to come to their churches or to other campuses around the country. We would go (students and professors) for weekend trips to places all over the United States to share what was happening and to give our testimonies. Miracles happened, and lives were changed all over the country as a result. And other Christian colleges and universities began to report similar outpourings of the Holy Spirit on their campuses. It was a faith-strengthening, life-changing experience that I'll never forget, and I will never be the same because of having been there. I'm so thankful that I was there to experience such an outpouring of the Holy Spirit. Let it happen again in this place, Lord!

(Beverley Brown Robb)

Asbury College President Dennis Kinlaw understood this was a legitimate revival—a true movement of God—and told a reporter, "The only way I know how to account for this is that last Tuesday morning, at about 20 of 11, the Lord Jesus walked into Hughes Auditorium, and He's been there ever since, and you've got the whole community paying tribute to his presence."[1] A student alumnus described the sacredness of the atmosphere as he stepped into chapel that Tuesday morning, saying it felt as if he were standing on holy ground.[2]

This miraculous anointing of the Holy Spirit lasted 185 hours nonstop (more than seven days). Intermittently, it continued for weeks. Ultimately, it spread to college campuses and churches across the United States and into foreign countries.

February 3, 1970, was a life-changing day for me. It was a long time ago. For many years after graduation, I didn't set foot in Wilmore, Kentucky. It's a long way from The Woodlands, Texas, and I was busy starting a new church and starting a family. But in recent years, as a trustee of Asbury Theological Seminary, I've had the opportunity to travel to Wilmore twice a year for seminary board meetings. When I'm back, I often sneak across the street to the college to slip into Hughes Auditorium and just sit there a few minutes to reflect on God's goodness . . . to remember the day God's Spirit touched my life. For me, it will always be a sacred place.

All through history, certain places have stood out as special, places we identify with God's presence. Zion is an actual hill in Jerusalem just outside the walls of the Old City of Jerusalem. But the terms Mount Zion and Zion in Scripture encompass the *entirety* of God's holy city of Jerusalem—from the Old City to the City of David, from the Temple Mount to the many hills that surround Jerusalem.

Zion is loved by Israel because it is where the Hebrew people have encountered the presence of God throughout much of their history. It is the place where Abraham prepared to sacrifice his son Isaac in an act of obedience to God. It is the place where King David established his fortress and where he placed the Ten Commandments given to Moses on Sinai. It is the place where David's son, King Solomon, built the first temple. Mount Zion is indeed a holy place—God's chosen dwelling place. It is the place where the children of Israel *connect* with Yahweh—the God of Abraham, Isaac, and Jacob.

Connection points are important in our lives. We are physical beings—creatures of time and space—so there is within us a yearning for a tangible connection to the things that have great meaning for us. We all have those special connection points we like to revisit—the little cafe where we first met our spouse, the family farm where our grandparents grew up, the town we were born and reared in—and can anyone say *high school reunion*? We revisit these places to reexperience the memories that are so special to us.

For the people of Israel, Zion is that connection point. Mount Zion represents the place of God's presence. It's not so much the physicality of the place, but the *spirituality* of the place that has such great meaning. God doesn't reside exclusively in the Temple, nor in a shrine nor on an altar. No. More than anyone, the Hebrew people have understood the *omnipresence* of God's nature.

A simple definition of *omnipresence* is "God is everywhere at once." (*Omni* is the Latin root word for "all.") God is present everywhere . . . all the time. Throughout history human beings have had difficulty comprehending an omnipresent God. That's why they worshiped idols. They wanted gods they could see and feel and touch—gods they could understand and control—gods made by their own hands, such as the gods of Baal and Pan. And, as we have learned in our journey together, the God of Abraham—the one we call the Lord God Yahweh—is *not* that kind of god.

Limited by neither time nor space, *God was everywhere the Israelites went.* He spoke from a mountainside thicket to Abraham and Isaac, and he called to Moses from a burning bush. His hand delivered the plagues of Egypt, stirred the pillar of fire in the wilderness, parted the Red Sea, and provided manna and water in the desert. God went before his people into the Promised Land. He poured down his fire upon an altar on Mount Carmel and spoke to the disciples from a bright cloud on Mount Tabor. *Everywhere the Israelites went, they discovered God was with them.* Israel's beloved King David, a man of poetry and war, knew this to be an absolute truth. Half of the 150 psalms are attributed to David, and he wrote extensively about God's omnipresence. In Psalm 139 he marvels:

> *Where can I go from your Spirit?*
> *Where can I flee from your presence?*
> *If I go up to the heavens, you are there;*
> *if I make my bed in the depths, you are there.*
> *If I rise on the wings of the dawn,*
> *if I settle on the far side of the sea,*
> *even there your hand will guide me,*
> *your right hand will hold me fast.*
> *If I say, "Surely the darkness will hide me*
> *and the light become night around me,"*

even the darkness will not be dark to you;
the night will shine like the day,
for darkness is as light to you.
(Psalm 139:7-12)

As David contemplates how God knows him inside and out, he wonders where he might go to hide from the Lord. Heaven, hell, east, west, the far side of the ocean—it doesn't matter. The Lord is already there. And what about the darkness of the night? David understood that even the darkness could not hide him, "for darkness is as light to you." God is in the midst of all his creation—from the tiniest atom to the vastness of the universe: "'Can anyone hide from me in a secret place? / Am I not everywhere in all the heavens and earth?' / says the LORD" (Jeremiah 23:24 NLT).

God reveals his presence uniquely to each one of us. Moses found God in fire and clouds on a mountain (Exodus 24:15-18). Elijah found God in the silence outside a cave (1 Kings 19:11-13). Silence is a good place to start. Psalm 46:10 tell us to be still and know that he is God. When we become still and seek God's presence with all of our senses, it is amazing how many ways we discover him—not just in our most profound moments but in our daily lives. British author and lay theologian C. S. Lewis wrote, "We may ignore, but we can nowhere evade, the presence of God. The world is crowded with Him. He walks everywhere *incognito*."[3] If we take time to be still, if we pay close attention, God faithfully reveals himself—in a sunrise, in the pounding of the surf, in the healing after a storm, in the music of worship, in the smile of a stranger, and even in the rain.

There is a touching story by Nancy Miller chronicled in the book *Chicken Soup for the Christian Family Soul* about a little girl named Danae Blessing who was born on a rainy afternoon in March 1991. Born prematurely through an emergency C-section, she was only twelve inches long and weighed one pound. The physicians told her parents that she would most likely not live long; and that if she did survive, she would suffer from a nightmarish list of disabilities. Danae's heartbroken father suggested they begin making plans for a funeral. But her mother, Diana, refused. She was determined her little girl would not only survive but that she would thrive and would one day go home with them. Danae clung to life, day after rainy day, as if willed by her mother's determination. Her parents prayed fervently for God to stay close to their precious little girl. Danae improved slowly as the months passed; and four months after she was born, she was able to go home, just as her mother had predicted.

Five years later, Danae was a vigorously healthy and feisty young girl with an unquenchable zest for life. In 1996, on a hot summer afternoon in Irving, Texas, Danae was at the ballpark with her mother, watching her brother play baseball. As she sat on her mother's lap, the usually talkative little girl suddenly became quiet. "Do you smell that?" she asked her mother. Diana took a moment to smell the air. A summer thunderstorm was approaching—the air smelled like rain. "Yes," Diana replied to her daughter, "it smells like rain." Little Danae hugged herself and told her mother, "No. It smells like *him*. It smells like God when you lay your head on His chest." In that moment, Diana knew that God had indeed stayed close to her little girl all those months in the hospital. And Danae knew it too.[4]

The Israelites understood that God is not limited by time or space and he *is* everywhere. But they also understood a deeper truth. The Lord God, Yahweh, the omniscient (*all-seeing*), omnipresent God, had a heart for his people. That connection started a long time ago. From the moment Adam and Eve fled Eden, God pursued the children he desperately loved. Throughout the centuries he went behind them, went before them, and drew alongside them, calling them back into relationship with him. Calling them into covenant—a binding relationship that will last forever, just as it was always meant to be. This is why the children of Israel love Zion. God chose to make his dwelling place there with them. For them, Mount Zion also represents the *heart* of God's presence.

One thousand years before the birth of Christ, King David captured Jerusalem from the fierce Canaanite tribe of the Jebusites. He moved his capitol to Jerusalem and lived in the fortress of Zion, which he named the City of David. And when he moved to Jerusalem, he brought with him the ark of the covenant.

Maybe you have heard of it . . . especially if you have seen the Indiana Jones film *Raiders of the Lost Ark*. The ark of the covenant is described in the Bible as a sacred container—a box—constructed of acacia wood. According to various texts within the Bible, the ark was built at the command of God and was covered in gold. Its lid was called the mercy seat; and above the mercy seat, at each end, sat two cherubim with their faces turned toward one another. Their outspread wings over the top of the ark formed the throne of God, while the ark itself was his footstool. The ark was fitted with rings and poles, which allowed it to be carried.

The ark of the covenant was an extravagantly decorated box; but more than that, it was a box that contained items that were greatly revered by the Hebrew people: the tablets of stone on which the Ten Commandments were inscribed; Aaron's rod, the staff of Moses' brother and high priest that demonstrated miraculous powers during the plagues of Egypt; and a jar that contained manna from the desert. The ark of the covenant was sacred to the people of Israel—its contents represented the holy, covenantal presence of God. So they carried the ark with them wherever they went. They carried it all during the forty years of wandering in the desert. Whenever they camped, the ark was placed in a special and sacred tent, called the Tabernacle. And when the Israelites crossed the Jordan River into the Promised Land, they carried the ark in front of them. During the Battle of Jericho, the ark was carried around the city once a day for seven days. And on the seventh day, the people blasted their trumpets and the walls fell. Victory was theirs.

King David brought the ark of the covenant to Mount Zion (2 Samuel 6:12-15), since it represented God's presence in the midst of his people. It reminded them of God's great acts of salvation, the Law given to Moses, God's provision during the wilderness years, and God's protection as they took possession of the Promised Land. When David's son King Solomon built the first Temple in the tenth century BC, the ark of the covenant was placed behind a curtain in a special inner room, called the Holy of Holies (1 Kings 8:1-6 MSG). This magnificent Temple was located in *Zion*—the place where God provided Abraham with a sacrifice in Isaac's stead—the home of the ark of the covenant and the sacred, desired dwelling place of God. What great joy! The words of the psalmist had come to pass:

> *He has founded his city on the holy mountain.*
> *The L*ORD *loves the gates of Zion*
> *more than all the other dwellings of Jacob.*
> (Psalm 87:1-2)

But Solomon, who was known and revered for his great wisdom, understood that while the Temple was indeed a special and holy place for the people of Israel, there was a danger in becoming too attached to a particular location, place, or building. As human beings, we can too easily limit God to that place. *Our hearts can become more attached to that place than to God.* So, in his prayer of dedication for the Temple, the Bible says:

> *Then Solomon stood before the altar of the L*ORD
> *in front of the whole assembly of Israel, spread*
> *out his hands toward heaven and said:*

"LORD, the God of Israel, there is no God like
you in heaven above or on earth below. . . .

"But will God really dwell on earth? The heav-
ens, even the highest heaven, cannot contain
you. How much less this temple I have built!"
(1 Kings 8:22-23, 27)

These were wise words from a wise King. Several hundred years later, in 587 BC, the Babylonians destroyed Jerusalem, including the Temple. They took most of the captured Jews to Babylon to serve as slaves. Psalm 137 is from this period; and to me, it is one of the most touching passages of Scripture:

By the rivers of Babylon we sat and wept
when we remembered Zion.
There on the poplars
we hung our harps,
for there our captors asked us for songs,
our tormentors demanded songs of joy;
they said, "Sing us one of the songs of Zion!"

How can we sing the songs of the LORD
while in a foreign land?
If I forget you, Jerusalem,
may my right hand forget its skill.
May my tongue cling to the roof of my mouth
if I do not remember you,
if I do not consider Jerusalem
my highest joy.
(Psalm 137:1-6)

What great sorrow! Their beloved city was in ruins. Their Temple was gone, but they still wanted to be back in Zion—*it was their spiritual home.*

Seventy years later, the Jews were released from captivity, and many returned to Jerusalem. The rebuilding of the second Temple was completed under the reign of King Darius in 516 BC and was magnificently reconstructed and expanded by King Herod, twenty years before the birth of Jesus.

Mount Zion and the Temple continued to represent the spiritual heart of the children of Israel. The Jews made joyful pilgrimages to the Temple in Jerusalem during the annual feasts. And the same holds true today. Wherever the Jews live, anywhere in the world, they want to be in Jerusalem. Especially at Passover.

But where is the ark of the covenant today? Gone. Lost. And Herod's great Temple? Destroyed by the Roman Emperor Titus in AD 70. But it wasn't destroyed completely. A portion of the Temple's platform, now known as the Western Wall, still stands and is revered greatly by the people of Israel. Foremost in their hopes and prayers is that the Temple will one day be rebuilt. To visit this place is a remarkably moving experience. People from around the world come to stand before the Western Wall to enter into intensely private moments of worship. Millions of hands are laid against the now-smooth surface of the wall, making a physical connection with the roots of their faith. Millions of prayers are whispered or written lovingly and tucked into the crevices of the wall's massive stones. If the stones could speak the prayers they contain, they would speak well into eternity. Millions of tears soak the surface of the wall as cheeks of young and old are pressed upon the stones—as if pressing into the very being of God. Waiting . . . hoping . . . praying.

The ancient stones of the Western Wall have more of a story to tell. Between the time of Herod's Temple and its destruction in AD 70, the Scriptures tell us something truly wondrous took place in the land of Israel. The omnipresent God of Abraham, Isaac, and Jacob put on the sandals of an itinerant rabbi and walked among his beloved children of Israel for thirty-three years. He laughed with them, wept with them, broke bread with them, taught them, healed them, and loved them. The presence of God, in the person of Jesus, had become intimately *personal*. Right there, on Mount Zion. He didn't reside in a gold-covered box behind a curtain in the Temple. He walked among his people.

But the religious leaders of the people—the Scribes, Pharisees, and Sadducees—had become so attached to the Temple they were blind to God's glory in their midst. They had forgotten Solomon's warning. Mount Zion and the Temple *symbolized* the presence of God; they didn't understand that Jesus *embodied* the presence of God.

Frustrated by this itinerant rabbi, the religious leaders challenged Jesus and asked him to prove his authority.

> *Jesus answered them, "Destroy this temple, and I will raise it again in three days."*
>
> *They replied, "It has taken forty-six years to build this temple, and you are going to raise it in three days?" But the temple he had spoken of was his body.*
>
> *(John 2:19-21)*

Sadly, the religious leaders and many of the people still didn't understand. They would not accept the deity of Jesus. In the days before his arrest and crucifixion, Jesus wept over Jerusalem, the place he loved . . . the place where his Father chose to dwell.

> *As he approached Jerusalem and saw the city, he wept over it and said, "If you, even you, had only known on this day what would bring you peace— but now it is hidden from your eyes. The days will come upon you when your enemies will build an embankment against you and encircle you and hem you in on every side. They will dash you to*

the ground, you and the children within your walls.
They will not leave one stone on another, because
you did not recognize the time of God's coming
to you."

(Luke 19:41-44)

What great sorrow! To miss the visitation of God is to miss the greatest blessing in our lives. We must never let our understanding of God's presence be confined to a building or a relic. The great spiritual truth Jesus taught is that the fullness of God's presence lives in him. *It's personal.* His Temple is now a *spiritual* temple that is established in the hearts of those who believe in him, and he is the cornerstone.

As you come to him, the living Stone—rejected by
humans but chosen by God and precious to him—
you also, like living stones, are being built into a
spiritual house. . . . For in Scripture it says:

"See, I lay a stone in Zion,
a chosen and precious cornerstone,
and the one who trusts in him
will never be put to shame."

(1 Peter 2:4-6)

Today, the Messiah—the living Lord—walks among us, visiting us in the sanctuaries of our daily lives. Whether in your home, your business, your church, in a neonatal intensive care unit, or even in a chapel in Wilmore, Kentucky, Jesus draws alongside you. He hears your prayers, weeps with your sorrows, exults in your joys, calls you to repentance, receives you into his kingdom, and brings you before his Father as he calls you his own. The omnipresent God of Abraham, Isaac, and Jacob put on human flesh and came to restore humankind to himself. He came for *you.* It's personal.

Mount Zion embodies the spiritual presence of God on earth. Jerusalem was, is, and always shall be God's beloved city. And Scripture reveals a wonderful glimpse of God's future plan for Zion, as seen in a vision of the apostle John:

> And he carried me away in the Spirit to a mountain great and high, and showed me the Holy City, Jerusalem, coming down out of heaven from God. It shone with the glory of God, and its brilliance was like that of a very precious jewel, like a jasper, clear as crystal. It had a great, high wall with twelve gates, and with twelve angels at the gates. On the gates were written the names of the twelve tribes of Israel. There were three gates on the east, three on the north, three on the south and three on the west. The wall of the city had twelve foundations, and on them were the names of the twelve apostles of the Lamb.
>
> I did not see a temple in the city, because the Lord God Almighty and the Lamb are its temple. The city does not need the sun or the moon to shine on it, for the glory of God gives it light, and the Lamb is its lamp. The nations will walk by its light, and the kings of the earth will bring their splendor into it. On no day will its gates ever be shut, for there will be no night there.
>
> (Revelation 21:10-14, 22-25)

It is no wonder that Zion holds a special place in our hearts. For both the people of Israel and followers of Christ, Jerusalem is holy ground. It's the connection point of our faith. It's why we are drawn to it. It's why so many believers want to set foot in the Holy Land at least once in their lifetime. With the psalmist of old, our spirits cry out:

> *How great is the L*ORD*,*
> > *how deserving of praise,*
> *in the city of our God,*
> > *which sits on his holy mountain!*
> *It is high and magnificent;*
> > *the whole earth rejoices to see it!*
> *Mount Zion, the holy mountain,*
> > *is the city of the great King!*
>
> > > > *(Psalm 48:1-2 NLT)*

Nothing gives my wife and me greater pleasure than to lead others in their personal pilgrimages to Israel. We have led many of these trips, and each time we approach Jerusalem we are overcome with emotion. On one such trip we traveled to Israel with members of our church choir. Shortly after the trip, I received a note from one of the sopranos, Jennifer Wilder Morgan, beautifully describing her experience:

> When we were in Israel and were approaching Jerusalem through the incredibly barren Judean Wilderness, our bus driver, Toby, began playing a song called "The Holy City." I had not heard that song before, but others on the bus began singing it. Hearing the words, I was absolutely overcome with emotion. Here I was, about to lay eyes on the place I had read about and studied about for most of my life. This was God's city . . . the God I love with all my heart,

and I began to understand the word "pilgrimage" in a new way. It is truly a return to my spiritual roots. Seeing the city for the first time was a moment that is hard to describe . . . so profound. When we exited the bus on Mount Scopus for a panoramic overlook of Jerusalem, I literally wept with joy.

(Jennifer Wilder Morgan)

Indeed, it is an emotional experience. Can you imagine hearing the lyrics below while overlooking the Holy City itself?

The Holy City

Last night I lay a sleeping,
There came a dream so fair,
I stood in old Jerusalem
Beside the temple there.
I heard the children singing,
And ever as they sang,
Methought the voice of angels
From Heav'n in answer rang;
Methought the voice of angels
From Heav'n in answer rang:—
Jerusalem! Jerusalem!
Lift up your gates and sing,
Hosanna in the highest
Hosanna to your King!

And then methought my dream was changed,
The streets no longer rang,
Hushed were the glad hosannas
The little children sang.
The sun grew dark with mystery,
The morn was cold and chill,

As the shadow of a cross arose
Upon a lonely hill,
As the shadow of a cross arose
Upon a lonely hill.
Jerusalem! Jerusalem!
Hark! how the angels sing,
Hosanna in the highest,
Hosanna to your King.

And once again the scene was changed,
New earth there seem'd to be,
I saw the Holy City
Beside the tideless sea;
The light of God was on its streets,
The gates were open wide,
And all who would might enter,
And no one was denied.
No need of moon or stars by night,
Or sun to shine by day,
It was the new Jerusalem,
That would not pass away,
It was the new Jerusalem,
That would not pass away.
Jerusalem! Jerusalem!
Sing, for the night is o'er!
Hosanna in the highest,
Hosanna for evermore!
Hosanna in the highest,
Hosanna for evermore![5]

The holy ground of Jerusalem—Mount Zion—truly is a physical connection with our omnipresent, personal God. And thanks to the life, death, and resurrection of our Messiah, Jesus Christ, we can stand on holy ground anywhere our feet take us. No matter where we are in the world, Christ sends his Spirit to dwell within the temples of our hearts, *for we are his desired dwelling place.* King David had it right. There is nowhere we can go where God is not present. Hallelujah!

Oh, dear Jerusalem, beside the tideless sea, in you I draw so near to God, and he draws near to me.

PEAK PERSPECTIVES: HERMON

In accordance with God's instructions (Leviticus 23:34, 42-43), the people of Israel made a pilgrimage to Jerusalem each fall to celebrate the harvest with Sukkot (also known as the Festival of Tabernacles or the Feast of Booths). This seven-day festival of joy and thanksgiving was designed to remember God's shelter and provision in the wilderness as the children of Israel traveled from Egypt to the Promised Land.

As part of the festival's daily ritual, water was poured from a golden pitcher on to an altar where sacrifices were made. This pouring of water was met with great music, celebration, and singing, a joyful expression of the crowd's glee that their labor was over, and rain was to come.[6]

It was on the last day of Sukkot that Jesus made an astonishing statement:

> *On the last and greatest day of the festival, Jesus stood and said in a loud voice, "Let anyone who is thirsty come to me and drink. Whoever believes in*

> *me, as Scripture has said, rivers of living water will*
> *flow from within them."*
> (John 7:37-38)

The intent of Jesus' message was clear. As water is the source of life, *Jesus* is the source of the water of *eternal* life. His entire ministry was spent in, on, and around the life-giving waters of Israel—the Jordan River, the Sea of Galilee, the Dead Sea, and even the Pool of Siloam. And all of these life-giving waters flowed from the sacred, snowcapped top of Mount Hermon.

Majestic Mount Hermon rises to a height of 10,000 feet and is a part of a mountainous ridge located between the border of Syria and Lebanon. In biblical times it was located in the land of Israel; and its name, *Hermon*, means "sacred." High places were holy places to the people of Israel, and Mount Hermon was the highest of the mountains. Its impressive snow-covered peak can be seen from the southern part of the region of Galilee, some sixty miles away. And Hermon was home to the equally majestic and fragrant Cedars of Lebanon, which covered its slopes in thick forests.

The cedars were a precious resource, sought after by many nations, and were harvested at God's instruction to build the great temple of Solomon in Jerusalem. It was believed these magnificent trees had been planted on Mount Hermon by God himself:

> *The trees of the LORD are well watered,*
> *the cedars of Lebanon that he planted.*
> *There the birds make their nests;*
> *the stork has its home in the junipers.*
> (Psalm 104:16-17)

Indeed, the Cedars of Lebanon are well-watered. With the spring snow melt on Hermon's uppermost slopes, torrents of icy, fresh water rush down the mountain, watering everything in their path. The waters feed great underground springs that nourish the land of Israel and serve as the source of the mighty Jordan River.

To this day the people of Israel consider the waters of this holy mountain to be life-giving waters to God's Holy Land. Flowing in a southerly direction from Hermon, the Jordan River is the primary source of the Sea of Galilee—a lush area teeming with life. The Sea of Galilee featured prominently in the ministry of Jesus. There, he made disciples of fishermen, preached from boats, walked on water, and calmed its violent storms.

Flowing through the Sea of Galilee, the Jordan River continues to travel south into the arid desert land of Israel. John the Baptist traveled this region, baptizing people in the waters of the Jordan, proclaiming, "I baptize you with water for repentance. But after me comes one who is more powerful than I, whose sandals I am not worthy to carry. He will baptize you with the Holy Spirit and fire" (Matthew 3:11). After Jesus' forty days of preparation in the desert, he came to John the Baptist to be baptized in the river Jordan. When Jesus rose from these sacred waters, the spirit of God alighted on him in the form of a dove, effectively beginning his earthly ministry.

During Jesus' ministry, he demonstrated his life-giving presence at the pools supplied by springs fed by Mount Hermon. He healed a paralyzed man by the steps of the Pool of Bethesda. The paralytic believed in the legend that the waters of the pool had healing properties but only if you were the first to enter. Since he could not walk on his own, he had never entered the pool. But when he met Jesus, he was healed only with the words, "Get up! Pick up your mat and walk" (John 5:8). Jesus also restored a blind man's sight by mixing his own saliva with mud, placing it on the man's eyes, and telling him to bathe in the Pool of Siloam.

The Jordan River continues its run south until it ends in the great salt sea—the Dead Sea—on the border of Jordan. The sea sits at the earth's lowest elevation on land—1,388 feet below sea level. And the Dead Sea is, virtually, dead. No life, no waves, no boats . . . only desolate stillness. The salt content is ten times that of the earth's ocean waters. Unlike the Sea of Galilee, which overflows with life, this sea is dead *because no water flows out of it.*

The waters from the cedar-forested, snowcapped mountain of Mount Hermon had everything to do with the ministry of Jesus. Our Lord Jesus Christ understood that abundant life occurs only when you receive what God pours into you and then let it flow out to others. Jesus lived this message every day, pouring out the love God gave him into everyone he met.

On the final day of the Feast of Booths on Mount Zion, Jesus said, "Let anyone who is thirsty come to me and drink. Whoever believes in me, as Scripture has said, rivers of living water will flow from within them" (John 7:37-38).

Five hundred years before the birth of Jesus, the prophet Zechariah spoke these words over Jerusalem about the days of the millennium, when Jesus returns to rule on earth:

> On that day there will be neither sunlight nor cold, frosty darkness. It will be a unique day—a day known only to the LORD—with no distinction between day and night. When evening comes, there will be light.
>
> On that day living water will flow out from Jerusalem, half of it east to the Dead Sea and half of it west to the Mediterranean Sea, in summer and in winter.
>
> The LORD will be king over the whole earth. On that day there will be one LORD, and his name the only name.
>
> (Zechariah 14:6-9)

With the return of our Lord, *all* the waters will be teeming with *abundant life*! Praise God from whom all blessings flow! Hallelujah!

ACKNOWLEDGMENTS

The idea for this book began almost fifty years ago, while I was an undergraduate at Asbury College. The pastor of the Methodist church I attended was a retired missionary from India, David A. Seamands. He was a gifted preacher and later became a popular author, writing primarily on the topic of emotional healing. Though I heard him preach many sermons during my time in that small college town, the one series I remembered was about mountains in the Bible. That became the genesis of this book, written decades later.

I want to thank Susan Salley, the associate publisher of Ministry Resources at Abingdon Press, who encouraged me to pursue this project. Also a word of deep appreciation is due to Lauren Arieux Bryan for her thorough assistance with detailed editing and resourcing. The reader will enjoy a better book because of her skill and involvement.

Without question the person I leaned on most during this process is my friend and author, Jennifer Wilder Morgan. Not only is she responsible for the devotionals at the end of each chapter, but she also contributed to this work as my writing assistant. Her keen imagination and spiritual insight helped to shape this book.

NOTES

Base Camp

1 Henry Wadsworth Longfellow, "Paul Revere's Ride," *The Atlantic Monthly*, archived January 1861 issue, https://www.theatlantic.com/magazine/archive/1861/01/paul-revere-s-ride/308349/.

Chapter 2. Sinai: Mount of God's Law

1 *The Ten Commandments*, produced and directed by Cecil B. DeMille (Hollywood, CA: Paramount Pictures, 1956).

2 "Amazing Grace," words by John Newton, 1779, *The United Methodist Hymnal* (Nashville: The United Methodist Publishing House, 1989), 378.

3 "Amazing Grace," *The United Methodist Hymnal*, 378.

Chapter 3. Carmel: Mount of Decision

1 Robert Frost, "The Road Not Taken," *Mountain Interval* (New York: Henry Holt and Co., 1916), 9, http://www.gutenberg.org/files/29345/29345-h/29345-h.htm#THE_ROAD_NOT_TAKEN.

2 Charlotte Buxton, "What on Earth Is a Mugwump?," in *Oxford Dictionaries Blog*, a blog by Oxford Dictionaries, April 27, 2017, https://blog.oxforddictionaries.com/2017/04/27/what-is-a-mugwump/.

3 Nell Ivin Painter, "Truth, Sojourner (1799–26 November 1883)," *American National Biography*, February 2000, http://www.anb.org/view/10.1093/anb/9780198606697.001.0001/anb-9780198606697-e-1500706.

Peak Perspectives: Masada

4 "Archaeology in Israel: Masada Desert Fortress," Jewish Virtual Library, accessed April 23, 2019, https://www.jewishvirtuallibrary.org/masada-desert-fortress.

5 Flavius Josephus, *The Wars of the Jews*, trans. William Whiston, Project Gutenberg ebook, last updated August 3, 2013, http://www.gutenberg.org/files/2850/2850-h/2850-h.htm.

Chapter 4. Beatitudes: Mount of Blessings

1 "The Continental Divide in Colorado," The Adventure Company, November 30, 2016, https://www.theadventurecompany.com/continental-divide-in-colorado/.

2 Jerome Murphy-O'Connor, *The Holy Land: An Oxford Archaeological Guide from Earliest Times to 1700*, 5th Ed. On Kindle (New York: Oxford University Press, 2008), 317.

3 William G. Carter, "Double Image," *No Box Seats in the Kingdom: Sermons for the Sundays After Pentecost (Last Third) Cycle B, Gospel Texts* (Lima: CSS Publishing, 1996), 90.

4 Frederick Buechner, *The Longing for Home: Recollections and Reflections* (New York: HarperCollins, 1996), 113 of 181, ebook.

5 Buechner, 137 of 181, ebook.

Peak Perspectives: Olivet

6 "Insulas," That the World May Know with Ray Vander Laan, accessed April 26, 2019, https://www.thattheworldmayknow.com/insulas.

Chapter 5. Tabor: Mount of Transfiguration

1 *The Bucket List*, directed by Rob Reiner (Burbank, CA: Warner Bros. Pictures, 2007).

2 "Ancient Caesarea Philippi," Bible History Online, accessed April 26, 2019, https://www.bible-history.com/biblestudy/caesarea -philippi.html.

3 William Steuart McBirnie, *The Search for the Twelve Apostles, Revised Edition* (Carol Stream, IL: Tyndale House, 2008).

4 "The Persecution Under Nero in Which Paul and Peter Were Honored at Rome with Martyrdom in Behalf of Religion," BibleHub, accessed April 27, 2019, https://biblehub.com/library /pamphilius/church_history/chapter_xxv_the_persecution _under_nero.htm.

5 Grant R. Osborne, "Mark 9:2-13, Jesus's Glory and Majesty Disclosed," *Mark*, Teach the Text Commentary Series (Grand Rapids: Baker Publishing Group, 2014), 152-157.

6 Soren Kierkegaard, *Soren Kierkegaard's Journals and Papers*, Vol. 1, A-E, ed. and trans. Howard V. Hong and Edna H. Hong (Bloomington, IN: Indiana University Press, 1967), 467.

7 *Hacksaw Ridge*, directed by Mel Gibson (Santa Monica, CA: Summit Entertainment, 2016).

8 *universal*

9 "The Apostles' Creed, Traditional Version," *The United Methodist Hymnal* (Nashville: The United Methodist Publishing House, 1989), 881.

Peak Perspectives: Calvary

10 Rabbi Reuel Dillon, "The Tunic of God," Synagogue Chavurat HaMashiach, accessed April 25, 2019, https://www.messianic spokane.com/terumah-thetunicofgod.

Chapter 6. Zion: Mount of God's Presence

1 "A Revival Account Asbury 1970," *The Forerunner*, March 31, 2008, http://forerunner.com/forerunner/X0585_Asbury_Revival_1970 .html.

2 Hannah Schultz and Aaron Evans, "A School of Revival," *The Asbury Collegian*, September 25, 2015, http://www.theasbury collegian.com/2015/09/a-school-of-revival/.

3 C. S. Lewis, *Letters to Malcolm: Chiefly on Prayer* (New York: HarperCollins, 2017), 101.

4 Jack Canfield et al., "The Smell of Rain," in *Chicken Soup for the Christian Family Soul: Stories to Open the Heart and Rekindle the Spirit* (Deerfield Beach, FL: Health Communications, 2000), 20–22.

5 "The Holy City," Words by Frederick E. Weatherly, 1892, *The Cyber Hymnal*, #2521, Hymnary.org, https://hymnary.org/hymn /CYBER/2521.

Peak Perspectives: Hermon

6 Wayne Stiles, "The Pool of Siloam—Connecting Sukkot and the Messiah," from the series "Connecting the Bible and Its Lands to Life", Bible.org, October 29, 2012, https://bible.org /seriespage/13-pool-siloam-connecting-sukkot-and-messiah.